DEALING CREATIVELY WITH DEATH

A Manual of Death Education
and Simple Burial
Fourteenth Edition, Revised and Updated

by Ernest Morgan

edited by *Jenifer Morgan*

Upper Access, Inc.
Book Publishers
PO Box 457, Upper Access Road
Hinesburg, Vermont 05461
http://www.upperaccess.com

Cataloging-in-Publication Data

Morgan, Ernest, 1905 -

Dealing creatively with death: a manual of death education and simple burial / by Ernest Morgan: edited by Jenifer Morgan — 14th rev. ed.

p.   cm.

ISBN 0-942679-24-5 : $14.95

1. Death—Handbooks, manuals, etc. 2. Burial—Handbooks, etc.

3. Funeral rites and ceremonies—Handbooks, manuals, etc.

I. Morgan, Jenifer. II. Title.

BD444.M658   2001

306.9—dc20   00-108031

Cover by Betsy Lampe

ISBN 0-942679-24-5   LC No. **00-108031**

TABLE OF CONTENTS

Why death education?; The growth of death education; About the death educator; Death education for children; The challenge of man-made death; Other man-made deaths; Life after death; How to go about death education; Application of the remaining chapters; Endnotes and Bibliography

A personal experience in home care; My daughter Jenifer's comments; Stages of dying [Denial and isolation; Anger; Bargaining; Depression; Acceptance]; Unfinished business; Deciding about home care; Help for home care; The hospice movement [What is hospice?; Hospice services; More facts about hospice; To locate the nearest hospice]; Pain Control; Nutrition; A caution; Alzheimer's disease; Acquired Immunodeficiency Syndrome—AIDS; The dying child; General comments on dying; Endnotes and Bibliography

Cultural barriers to grieving; The process of grieving; My own experience with grief; Group support in bereavement; Children and grief; The death of a child; Suicide survivors; AIDS survivors; Special issues for bisexual or homosexual men; Other situations of bereavement; Support groups and professional help; Good physical care; Avoid the use of drugs; Catastrophic loss; Bereavement overload; How death illuminates life—an example; Endnotes and Bibliography

INTRODUCTION TO THE FOURTEENTH EDITION

Important changes have occurred in the fields of death and dying since the thirteenth edition of the *Manual* was published in 1994, and the cost of funerals continues to rise much more rapidly than the consumer price index. This edition offers new information for coping with this problem and solid counsel in dealing with pre-need sales, which have been rapidly increasing.

The AIDS epidemic affects the process of bereavement, care for the dying, and arrangements for disposition of the body. This is dealt with in Chapter 3, "Bereavement;" Chapter 2, "Living with Dying;" and Chapter 5, "Simple Burial and Cremation." References for further information are given.

The shocking increase in youth suicide is discussed in Chapter 4, "The Right to Die," looking briefly at causes and offering suggestions for prevention and further study.

Less well known is the rapid increase in the number of organ transplants. For example, in 1982 there were 103 heart transplants in the United States. In 1999 that number had increased to 2,185. New networks have developed to coordinate organ donations in both the United States and Canada, and new laws have been passed providing guidelines. These changes, and the sharply increased need for organ donations, are discussed in Chapter 8, "How the Dead Can Help the Living," and Appendix 8, "Anatomical Gifts."

The number of hospices in America has been growing rapidly, and there are now about 2,500 of them in the U.S. Chapter 2, "Living with Dying," reflects the changes taking place in the hospice movement, including use of hospice care for patients with Alzheimer's disease.

Chapter 3, "Bereavement," has been substantially rewritten to reflect our growing understanding of grieving, and the growth potential it contains.

Rapid changes in law are taking place in response to the medical ability to prolong life in the dying and the growing struggle, as a result, to avoid needless suffering and expense. The latest information on the rights of patients and families, and how to implement these rights, is contained in Chapter 4, "The Right to Die," and Appendix 4, "Living Will."

As with each previous edition for the past thirty-eight years, the book has been thoroughly revised, to keep it what it has always been, a small encyclopedia combining time-tested wisdom with timely relevance and up-to-date sources of information. We are grateful for the suggestions of our readers and invite them to send us criticisms and information, which may be useful in future editions.

Of the many people who helped me over the years with writing projects, I count Ernest Morgan as *primus inter pares*—first among equals.

In the early 1960s, when I was preparing *The American Way of Death,* I ran across his *Manual of Simple Burial*—a brilliant little volume of advice to the hapless survivor who wants to avoid the full-fig funeral with all the costly trimmings, decreed by the undertakers as being what they are pleased to call "the standard American funeral."

Once, years ago, Ernest Morgan and I shared a flight from Seattle to Oakland. In the course of our conversation I asked what motivated him to continue active in the field of death education and simple burial. He looked out the window for a while, then he said, "There are three reasons. First, working in this field is contributing to my own emotional maturity—my acceptance of death, my appreciation of life, and my concern for my fellow beings.

"Second, I desire social change and a more humane and cooperative society. At no time are people more prone to think about life values, and more open to change, than at a time of death or in thinking about death. This is a strategic time to influence them creatively, and combat what is phony, exploitative, and ostentatious in American life.

"Third, the *Manual* is making money for the Arthur Morgan School!"

Mr. Morgan and I became firm pen pals and have corresponded for three decades. He was immeasurably helpful in giving guidance and practical advice when I was writing *The American Way of Death*, and for years thereafter as we fought in our respective communities what one writer called "the battle of the Bier Barons."

Unlike the *Manual*, my own book does not deal with philosophic approaches to death and dying, but with the funeral industry. In his review of *The American Way of Death*, Evelyn Waugh wrote that "the trouble with Miss Mitford is that she has no stated attitude towards death." I wrote my sister Nancy, who was a friend of Waugh's: "Tell Evelyn that I *do* have an attitude towards death. I'm against it." (When I told Ernest Morgan this, he commented in his wry, dry fashion, "Better not abolish death. If we do, people will need a government permit to have a baby!")

In contrast with early editions of the *Manual*, this expanded version, while retaining its useful information about memorial societies, bequeathal of remains to medical schools, etc., goes more deeply into the practical and philosophical concerns of death and dying.

His perceptive, humane views on these matters should provide great solace to the terminally ill and their families.

—*Jessica Mitford**
(1917 - 1996)

*Foreword originally written for the Twelfth Edition of this book

PREFACE / How This Book Happened

My father, Arthur E. Morgan, was an intensely creative man whose activities had a lasting impact in several areas of American life. He had long felt that American funeral practices could be simpler and more meaningful. In 1948 he formed the Burial Committee of the Yellow Springs Friends Meeting (Quaker) to study the matter in a systematic way.

After five years of study his committee evolved a plan whereby the meeting would care for its own dead, handling the paperwork, building the boxes, conveying the bodies to a crematory or medical school and arranging memorial services—all without professional assistance.

In 1953 I was drafted by the meeting to chair this committee. I had no special interest in the project but did not wish to avoid responsibility, so I accepted. After all, I thought, I am a grown man, I can probably handle a dead body as well as the next fellow.

During the five years of study no one in the meeting had died, but as soon as I became chairman they started dying! Then I discovered that what I had anticipated to be a disagreeable chore turned out to be a meaningful privilege—serving one's friends at a time of profound need. The plan worked well at small cost, and the memorial services became a comfort and an inspiration to all concerned.

Then, quite by accident, our little burial committee got nationwide publicity. Letters poured in, asking for information. Gosh, I thought, I can't answer all these letters; I'll mimeograph a few sheets to send these people. Then another thought occurred to me. A burial committee is fine for a close-knit rural group like ours, but in most situations a memorial society that works with funeral directors is more practical. I'd better include some information on memorial societies. So I started digging out this information. (There was no memorial society association then.)

A short time later my stepmother, Lucy Morgan, asked me to make arrangements for her to leave her body to the university's medical school. She was a thrifty soul. "I don't want my body wasted," she said. So I went and met Dr. Graves(!) who was dean of the anatomy department. Dr. Graves was (almost too) enthusiastic. "If only more people would do this! There's a serious shortage of bodies in many areas." So I saw that I'd better tell people about leaving their bodies to a medical school.

Another five years passed. Instead of a few sheets I had a 64-page book, *A Manual of Simple Burial*. It appeared in 1962, printed by Celo Press, a division of the Arthur Morgan School, which my wife and I were launching then. It was well received.

In 1963 another surprise. The Co-op League called a meeting to federate the memorial societies of the United States and Canada. Would I be a keynote speaker? I seemed to have become an authority. Soon I was on the board of the Continental Association of Funeral and Memorial Societies. Who was it who said, "There is a destiny that shapes our ends"?

The book sold well and helped support the school. New editions followed, each extensively revised. Howard Raether, then executive director of the National Funeral Directors Association, once asked me, "How come you change the book so much between editions?" All I could say was, "Times change, and new ideas and information keep coming."

One thing I learned was that people turn their backs on the idea of death and are thus inhibited from joining a memorial society or planning ahead. Death education is almost a prerequisite for coming to grips with the question. So with our sixth edition we changed the title to *A Manual of Death Education and Simple Burial.* Sales continued to grow.

In 1971 my first wife died of cancer after a long illness. During her final months I kept her at home, where her life could be filled with love and fellowship and music—our introduction to what is now called hospice. Another dimension was thus added to the *Manual.*

Looking back, I realize that much of the book came from my long life in a warm cohesive family where death was a repeated visitor, and from half a century in a small community where life and death were deeply shared. That was my university, which was supplemented by reading and by association with many knowledgeable people.

No one has benefitted more from reading this book than I have from writing it. As a child I was devoted to my father, a man of great strength and gentleness. Accepting his death was hard for me, and writing this *Manual* made it possible for me to face reality and accept his death and that of others whom I loved.

The *Manual* (now titled *Dealing Creatively with Death*) is no longer my book but belongs as well to a host of friends and scholars who have helped with it. In particular, my daughter, Jenifer, has done much of the research and writing for recent editions and has been my most faithful and exacting critic.

Proceeds from the book still go to the Arthur Morgan School.

—Ernest Morgan

INTRODUCTION / About Accepting Death

If we were to walk across the fields in summertime to some undisturbed spot and mark off a piece of ground—say, four feet square—and then examine this little area minutely, we would find an astonishing variety of life. There would be many species of plants, possibly a mouse's nest, and several small creatures. Then, resorting to a microscope, we could observe an incredible host of microorganisms functioning in association with the larger life forms. But we would not stop there. We would start digging, exploring for additional life underground. There, too, we would find insects, nematodes, earthworms of various kinds, and a fresh array of bacteria. Nor would we necessarily stop when we reached bedrock. If that rock happened to be Ohio limestone, there would be several hundred feet of dense fossil deposits laid down through millions of years, representing myriad species and astronomical numbers of individual lives.

In that little square of ground we would see an interdependent community of life in which birth and death are continuously taking place and in which diverse life forms shelter and nourish one another. Written in the rocks beneath would be the story of a similar process going back through eons of time.

Humankind is part of the ongoing community of nature on a world scale; it is subject to the same cycle of birth and death that governs all other creatures, and, like them, it is totally dependent on other life. Sometimes, in our high-rise apartments, our manicured suburbs, and our chromium plated institutions, we tend to forget this.

Our need is not to conquer nature but to live in harmony with it. This does not mean rejecting our technology, but it does mean controlling our numbers, quieting our egos, and simplifying our lifestyles.

Birth and death are as natural for us as for the myriad creatures in that little square of ground. When we have learned to accept ourselves as part of the community of nature, then we can accept death as part of the natural order of things.

We commonly act as if we, and those we love, are going to live forever. But we are wrong, for all must die—nor can we know when this will happen.

In our culture we tend to avoid the subject of death. This is unfortunate, for death is a normal and necessary part of life. Until we learn to face it honestly and accept it, we are not living at our best.

If we are to appreciate our fellows, if we are to live with patience, gentleness, and love, let us be about it today—for life is short.

1 DEATH EDUCATION

This chapter has three functions.

*First is to break the ice—for those who need to have it broken—and help
people think and talk about death more easily. Until they are able to do this
without feeling uncomfortable, they will have difficulty in benefiting from the
ensuing chapters.*

*Second is to review briefly the emergence of death education and to discuss
some of the ways in which it is strongly relevant to life, both of the individual
and of society.*

*Third, this chapter gives a brief overview of the rest of the book, suggesting
possible uses of the remaining chapters, and offering suggestions for persons
who may be leading classes or discussions on the topic.*

Why Death Education?

Death education is for everyone, because it relates not just to death but to
our feelings about ourselves and nature and the universe we live in. A prime
function of death education is to help us to think and feel deeply about the
meaning of life in its many relationships—to help mature our values. As
Abraham Maslow wrote after recovering from a heart attack, "The confrontation
with death—and the reprieve from it—makes everything look so precious, so
sacred, so beautiful that I feel more strongly than ever the impulse to live it, to
embrace it and to let myself be overwhelmed by it."[1] Confronting death
imaginatively through experience, reading, thinking, lectures, and discussions
often has the paradoxical effect of enriching life.

As we pass beyond the fear and avoidance of death so common in our
culture, we can learn to accept dying as an appropriate culmination of life. To
do this we need to be able to talk freely with our loved ones about death—both
our own and theirs, whether imminent or remote.

Death education does not avoid grief—and should not if it could— but it can
help us to cope with grief in a creative way, so that we may grow in the quality
of our lives. It can help us also to relate meaningfully to dying persons, and to
meet the social and emotional needs of the survivors— including ourselves.

Then, too, it can help us deal wisely with practical matters that must be faced
at time of death, thus avoiding unnecessary ostentation, suffering, and expense.

Death education is doubly valuable for those whose work brings them into frequent contact with dying, death, and/or bereavement. These include not only health professionals, counselors, and clergy, but also law enforcement, military, and disaster personnel who work with survivors of major loss and sudden death.

The Growth of Death Education

Forty years ago the subject of death was taboo in polite society, as sex had been in earlier days. In 1959 Dr. LeRoy Bowman's sociological study, *The American Funeral*, and Herman Feifel's *The Meaning of Death* cracked the barrier. In 1962 the first edition of my *Manual* appeared, followed in 1963 by Ruth Harmer's *The High Cost of Dying* and Jessica Mitford's bombshell, *The American Way of Death*. That same year the memorial societies emerged, largely under church leadership, as a united continent-wide movement.

In 1967 Earl Grollman's *Explaining Death to Children* was published, and in 1969 Elisabeth Kübler-Ross gave the movement fresh depth and impetus with her classic *On Death and Dying*, stressing the need for death education among health care professionals. Since that time, hundreds of books and thousands of articles have appeared.

In 1975 the Forum (now Association) for Death Education and Counseling was organized, giving form and substance to the movement, and grew to over one thousand members working professionally in the field. Thousands of schools and colleges have classes in death education. Many churches likewise conduct seminars and conferences on the subject. Important, too, it has become a significant topic in courses in sociology, psychology, health care disciplines, literature, law, art, biology, philosophy, religion, and consumer education.

Simultaneously, hospice programs began in the United States. The National Hospice Organization was formed in 1977 to provide national leadership in education, research, standard setting, and advocacy. Hospices now train thousands of volunteers and professionals to deal humanely with dying and death. See Chapter 2, "Living With Dying."

Clearly, death education has come into its own.

About the Death Educator

Educators and counselors need to have a deep understanding and acceptance of death and dying. It is this understanding, combined with personal experience, which qualifies one to teach. It is the ability to share this experience and understanding directly from the heart that makes a fine teacher.

Similarly, an important qualification—perhaps the most important qualification—for anyone to counsel bereaved persons is that the counselor can deal creatively with suffering and is able to reach out to and empathize with the person being counseled. Most such counselors—at least the good ones—have been drawn into the field by virtue of their own experience and what they have learned from it.

Such counseling, at its best, is a two-way experience in which the counselor as well as the counseled experiences growth. That is one of the rewards of being a counselor.

In recent years, arrangements have been made for the certification of counselors in this field, by the Association for Death Education and Counseling. See Appendix 2, "Organizations" for listing. But this does not remove the responsibility of the rest of us to assist in this area when occasion arises.

Death Education for Children

Children have more awareness of death than most of us realize. Fairy tales, movies, and television programs abound in death, as does the world of nature, which they see about them.

Herman Feifel comments that "The shaping impact of awareness of death is active at all levels."[2] By age two, children's play demonstrates an awareness of death. Children three to five years of age commonly see death as temporary and reversible. From about five to nine years of age the finality is recognized and children begin to understand that death is an inevitable part of life. At first they think of it as something that happens to others, but not to themselves; later they realize it will someday happen to them. By age ten, if not before, most children understand the reality of death as adults do.[3]

Acceptance of death as part of life needs to be incorporated into a child's normal activities at home and at school. On occasions of deaths in my own family, the children were kept close to the center of family life and given roles to carry out in family activities relating to the deaths. This gave comfort to the adults as well as to the children.

Although wildly emotional outbursts may be upsetting to children, adults should not try to conceal their emotions from their children. Naturalness and honesty are basic. The physical fact of death should be explained, and children should not be discouraged from touching dead things if they wish. It should be explained that dead things feel no pain, as children commonly have great fear of pain. It helps to explain that we are part of the world of nature and share with all other creatures the cycle of life and death. For each of us there is a time to be born, to grow and flourish, and then to die. Fears are lessened if the emphasis is on the beauty of life.

The Challenge of Man-Made Death

A major challenge to death education—and one of its greatest potentials for usefulness, is in confronting the issues of man-made death. The first of these—now happily diminishing (at this writing)—is the threat of nuclear war. The nations of the world do, however, own nuclear weapons with explosive power equal to fifteen thousand million tons of TNT, and these weapons are proliferating. The other wing of the nuclear threat is pollution, as millions of tons of radioactive waste, with a half-life of thousands of years, pile up from the manufacture of nuclear weapons and from the generating of nuclear power.

A second threat, as dangerous and difficult as the nuclear one, is the environmental crisis. During the last half century the world has lost half its arable land to erosion and desertification, while nearly trebling its human population. Each second of the day and night we are losing an acre of forest and adding three people to the population. The greenhouse effect is starting, the ozone layer is thinning, the pollution of air and water is rising, and the ocean phytoplankton, which produce two-thirds of the world's oxygen, is diminishing. Our present course, if unchanged, can lead to suffering and death beyond anything experienced in human history.

Death education can help us to confront and deal with both the threats of war and the crisis of the environment. It can help us also to cope with the tendency to despair. Commenting on the nuclear menace, sociologist Henrik Infield exclaimed, "If we're going to be blown up, let's be blown up doing something worthwhile!" In other words, we should accept the reality of the dangers that face us, then place our bets on life!

There are constructive ways in which we can deal with the prospect of human extinction. To take a hand in our own destiny, even on a tiny scale, improves our chances and, besides, gives us a sense of empowerment that is essential to our emotional well-being.

A teacher in Seattle once asked her students, "How many of you think there might be a nuclear war?" Hands were raised by every child but one. "And you, Sally, why aren't you expecting that?"

"Well, Mommy and Daddy are working for disarmament and I think they're going to win."

Human solidarity is important. For an old-timer like myself, there is a temptation to take refuge in the thought that I'm likely to be dead and gone before hell breaks loose. But I quickly reject this impulse as cowardly and take my stand with the young people who will inherit the future. We can't avoid our individual deaths, but we can try, by thoughtful and concerted action, to avoid the death of our civilization. This idea can give us inspiration and hope.

Other Man-Made Deaths

War and ecological disaster are not the only forms of man-made death that need to be dealt with openly. There are difficult social questions, such as capital punishment, abortion, euthanasia, smoking, accidental deaths, and suicide. Some of these issues are beyond the scope of this book, but euthanasia and suicide are dealt with at length in Chapter 4, "The Right to Die."

Life After Death

The continuity of biological life is obvious. Also evident is the continuity of cultural patterns and values. The continuity of the individual soul is an article of faith with most major religions of the world. Christianity, Judaism, and Islam hold the view that the soul maintains its ego individuality throughout eternity. In the East, Hinduism and Buddhism generally stress a series of reincarnations in different egos eventually leading to merging of the individual soul (Atman) into the cosmic soul (Brahman, or Nirvana).

The existence and nature of an afterlife has been inferred from presumed interactions with spirits of the dead (mediums, apparitions, spirit photographs and recordings, and possession, for example), and from apparently confirmed memories of previous incarnations. Recently, much attention has been given to evidence derived from "near death experiences" of people at or near death who revived. Elisabeth Kübler-Ross says she has spoken to more than a thousand such people, and Raymond Moody's *Life After Life* describes several such experiences in detail.

Some researchers emphasize the lack of conclusive proof for religious dogmas and for the theory that life after death explains these phenomena. Others suggest that the idea of an afterlife explains the various phenomena more readily than other theories do. While ideas about an afterlife are many and varied, most hold that death is a transition to a new state of being; and that the quality of that state depends at least in part on how we lived on earth and the state of our spiritual development.

How to Go About Death Education

First of all, consider the makeup and needs of the class. How old are the students? Is it made up of hospice volunteers who need to relate to dying persons? Is it a group of health professionals, and if so, at what level? Is it an adult seminar including people with problems of grief and loss? Is it for church people considering plans for their own last rites and arrangements, or perhaps planning a support group for assisting bereaved families?

This has a bearing on the topics to be included and what emphasis to give to each. Teachers need to be sensitive to the particular needs they are dealing with and the feelings that may be evoked. It helps to circulate a questionnaire to the members of the class at the outset, including such questions as "Why are you taking this course?" "What was your most significant experience with death?" "Do you have any special death-related experiences that you bring to the class?"

In all class discussions and role playing, participation should be voluntary and students should not be pressed for answers. Offering alternative assignments can allow students to decide whether or not to approach an emotionally difficult subject. Books containing teaching resources are listed at the end of this chapter.

Application of the Remaining Chapters

Each chapter of this Manual presents a topic or topics that may be included in a syllabus.

"Living with Dying," Chapter 2, stressing home care for the terminally ill, will be of special interest to hospice workers and other health care personnel. Churches may use it to help in supporting home care for parishioners. Members of funeral consumer organizations (formerly known as memorial societies) and others will be interested in planning to meet their families' needs. Family life courses will also find this material helpful.

"Bereavement," Chapter 3, is an essential topic for all of us, as experience of loss is universal. Hospice workers are committed to bereavement support. Every counselor, clergyman, and health care worker needs the information this chapter provides. Churches will find it helpful in encouraging congregational support of the bereaved in the church community.

"The Right to Die," Chapter 4, is of special interest to persons facing terminal illness within their families and to those who wish to make provision in advance to ensure that they will have some control over their own deaths. Likewise it is of interest to all persons involved in health care, including, of course, hospice workers. Students of law and philosophy also will find this frequently controversial presentation interesting. This chapter deals also with the increasingly urgent problem of suicide and the role of the teacher in dealing with this problem.

"Simple Burial and Cremation," Chapter 5, presents the philosophy and practice of planning for and handling a death in the family in a simple manner—information every family should have. Professionals and volunteers who work with the dying can be of great service in making this information available. Church leaders, too, will want this information to meet the needs of their religious communities. As with funeral consumer organizations, this topic should be included in consumer education.

"Funeral Consumer Organizations," Chapter 6, should be understood by all who work with death and dying—or who expect to die someday! They have a unique role in assisting families who desire simplicity and economy in funeral arrangements.

"Death Ceremonies," Chapter 7, is very important information in meeting the social and emotional needs of survivors at a time of death. This chapter has been included at the request of several readers who felt that alternative types of ceremonies would better meet these needs. It is also useful to church people and others who may be concerned with planning a service. Special attention is given to memorial services.

"How the Dead Can Help the Living," Chapter 8, encourages people to make anatomical gifts at the time of death, and tells how to plan accordingly. This is an urgent concern at the present time, of special relevance to health professionals, biologists, and lawyers.

Extensive material on death education, in addition to the books listed at the end of this chapter, is available. See Appendix 1.

ENDNOTES

[1]From a letter to Dr. Rollo May as it appeared in *Love and Will*, by Rollo May. New York: W.W. Norton, 1969. Used with permission.

[2]Herman Feifel, "The Meaning of Death in American Society," in *Death Education,* by Donald Irish and Betty Green. Cambridge, MA: Schenkman Publishing Company, 1971, p. 5.

[3]De Spelder & Strickland, *The Last Dance: Encountering Death & Dying*, Mountain View, CA: Mayfield Publishing Co., 1992. Includes a good summary of developmental studies of children's concepts of death.

BIBLIOGRAPHY/CHAPTER 1
(A few of many. For a wider selection, see Appendix 1.)

Awareness of Death: Preparation for Living, Donald P. Irish. Religious Education Committee, Friends General Conference, 1502-B Race St., Philadelphia, PA 19102, 1976.

Death: Current Perspectives, Edwin S. Schneidman. Palo Alto, CA: Mayfield Publishing Co., 1980. Concepts of death: death as a social disease, demography of death, determination of death, participants of death, survivors of death, life after death, self-destruction; bibliography. Highly recommended.

Death: The Final Stage of Growth, Elisabeth Kübler-Ross. Englewood Cliffs, NJ: Prentice-Hall, Inc., 1975. Essays on the philosophies of death and afterlife of Hinduism and Buddhism, practices of Judaism and Alaskan Indians, attitudes of hospital personnel, and personal experiences of death as a growthful experience from the perspective of both the dying and the bereaved.

Ethnic Variations in Dying, Death & Grief, D. Irish, K. Lundquist, and V. Nelsen, eds. Bristol, PA: Taylor & Francis, Inc., 1993. A presentation of the beliefs about death, burial, and mourning practices of various ethnic and religious groups with illustrative episodes.

Healing into Life and Death, Stephen Levine. New York: Anchor Press/ Doubleday, 1987. Might be considered a refinement of *Who Dies?* with profound commentary and guided meditations of healing grief and disease.

National Center for Death Education, Mt. Ida College, 777 Dedham St., Newton Center, MA 02159. Provides print and visual audiovisual materials on all aspects of death, dying, and bereavement. 617-928-4649 (URL: http// www.mountida.edu/ncde1.html.

New Meanings of Death, Herman Feifel. New York: McGraw Hill, 1977. Outstanding anthology, including articles by Kastenbaum, Bluebond-Langner, Schneidman, Weisman, Garfield, Saunders, Kelly, Kalish, Leviton, Lifton, Simpson, Gutman, and Shaffer and Rodes.

The Psychology of Death, 2nd ed., Robert Kastenbaum. New York: Springer Publishing, 1992. A critical review of recent findings, trends, and concepts about death and death attitudes. Every aspect of death is systematically covered.

The Social Reality of Death: Death in Contemporary America, Kathy Charmaz. Reading, MA: Addison-Wesley Publishing Co., 1980. A clear and comprehensive college textbook covering varied approaches to death, dying, ethics, death in medical settings, "extraordinary death," suicide, the funeral industry, and grief and mourning. Highly recommended.

2   LIVING WITH DYING

In this chapter I tell of my experience in caring for a dying patient at home and discuss how to relate to a dying person in a positive way. Also discussed are group support for the family of a dying person and how to relate to a dying child. These things are described as part of the hospice concept and the growing hospice movement. Appendix 3 reviews financial help available for home care. I am indebted to friends in the Hospice movement, especially Donna O'Toole, of Compassion Books, for help with this chapter.

A Personal Experience in Home Care

I had never heard of the hospice philosophy in 1971 when my first wife, Elizabeth, was dying of cancer, but my daughter and I had the basic concept. It was Elizabeth's wish to spend her last weeks at home, so we brought her there.

Arrangements were not complicated. My daughter got instructions at the hospital and then passed them along to me—how to give shots, change bedding, give baths, and take care of toilet needs. How to take pulse and temperature we already knew, and keeping a hospital chart was a simple routine. We borrowed a hospital bed, an over-the-bed table, and a commode chair, and contrived a stand for the intravenous fluids from a sturdy music rack. Such incidentals as a rubber sheet and bedpan were purchased or borrowed. When intravenous medication was prescribed, a nurse from the health department came and started it. All in all, it wasn't as difficult as we had expected and was easier because we loved the patient. The chief requirement was the desire and willingness to do it.

We had a good working relationship with the doctor, who talked on the phone with us every couple of days, made medical decisions, and prescribed medicines. Elizabeth experienced chronic pain, controlled by shots whenever she called for them, as instructed by the doctor. At that time there was no hospice organization, but we had strong community support. Friends ran errands and did shopping for us and gave a hand wherever needed.

The best part about home care was that my wife was surrounded by loving family members and friends. She loved music and was a fine musician, so by her bed we put an FM radio that brought in several National Public Radio stations. (Bless NPR!) She tried to have a visit with each of her students before she died, and family and friends from far and near came to see her. Some sang for her—folk songs and gospel hymns. Often they embraced her. It was a warmly human situation.

Elizabeth's acceptance of death was helped by turning much of her attention outside herself. As her strength permitted, she talked with the young people she knew, discussing their problems and plans. I recall an evening at the hospital, before she came home. Talking with the doctor, she said, "There's a little girl at school to whom I've promised the lead in next year's operetta, and she needs it so badly! I've just got to have another year." The doctor had tears in his eyes when he left the room, and he put her back on chemotherapy for one more try.

Elizabeth accepted the prospect of death calmly, almost cheerfully, but fought hard for life. We prepared "green drinks" and other things said to cause remissions, and none of us gave up hope until the very end. We knew that she was going to die, however, and talked about it frankly. Elizabeth told me shortly before she died how much it meant to her that we were able to accept her death. Some dying persons whose families would not accept their death or talk about it have written me, a stranger, to fill this void. Her actual death was peaceful, as she quietly stopped breathing.

Elizabeth had been afraid her death might upset the students at the Arthur Morgan School, with whom she had a very close relationship. Accordingly we prepared together a talk, which I gave them, discussing life and death. They received it thoughtfully and seemed to benefit from it. One of these students, a few years later, died of bone cancer following the amputation of both legs. The family's psychologist told me afterward that the buoyant and understanding spirit he maintained directly reflected his experience of Elizabeth Morgan's death.

My Daughter Jenifer's Comments

"When we realized in 1971 that Mother was losing her two-year battle with cancer, I was glad to be able to bring my two children, then ten and twelve years old, and help take care of her. Dad bought an old house trailer and set it up for us nearby, and I went to the hospital and learned general practical nursing.

"We shared the general housework and physical care of Mother, while I did most of the cooking and each evening gave her a back rub, which seemed to be especially comforting. I had time to go out occasionally with friends and participate in a peer counseling support group. Through this, one friend learned of the struggle I was having caring for one of my children, whose personality clashed with Mother's, and she invited him to stay with her family for a while. That helped a lot, though often I felt torn in the evenings between spending time with the children or giving the special care that would ease Mother's nights.

"Cooking presented its own problems. Mother's tastes and needs were simple—she especially loved lamb chops and baked custard—but one effect of the cancer was to upset the digestive system so that nothing really tasted good or digested easily. Thus I found myself feeling inadequate in caring for her, despite knowing better.

"The control of pain presented some difficulties, too. The medicines we used tended to make Mother groggy, so she tried to use as little as possible, torn between full but painful consciousness and partial loss of selfhood. The medicines were given by shots, and this in itself became increasingly painful to her. It was a problem we never fully resolved. [Since 1971, great improvements have been made in pain control.]

"Through it all, Mother had a remarkably buoyant and outgoing spirit. Dad and I both felt that our investment of time and energy in home care was richly rewarded in family closeness, strength gained, and love expressed."

STAGES OF DYING

The five stages of dying listed below were postulated by Elisabeth Kübler-Ross in her landmark book *On Death and Dying*. They are not to be taken as gospel, however, as she herself points out. They describe emotional responses commonly experienced by dying persons, but may be experienced very differently depending upon a person's particular illness, age, sex, personality, religious orientation, and situation.

In relating to a dying person it is helpful to realize that these reactions are normal and should be accepted. Not all of them will necessarily appear, nor will they necessarily appear in the order listed. No one should be expected or pushed to experience any of them, nor judged lacking for not experiencing one or more, including acceptance. Each person experiences death in a unique way.

A person who, through reading, discussion, and reflection has accepted the reality and universality of death may soften or eliminate the negative reactions. That is one of the values of death education. Similarly, negative feelings often reflect the inability of those around a patient— family, friends, and caretakers—to accept death. If others can accept the impending death and continue to relate warmly to the patient as a human being, he or she will also be able to accept the situation more easily.

These are the stages as set forth by Kübler-Ross:

Denial and isolation are often the first response to a terminal diagnosis. The patient will doubt the diagnosis or be convinced of the certainty of recovery. This can help to gain time for the person to assimilate the magnitude of the impending changes ("terror management"). This is different from the element of hope for recovery or reprieve, which remains and is helpful even when death has been accepted.

Anger usually accompanies acceptance of the diagnosis and may be directed at medical personnel, family, friends, oneself, and God. Outwardly or inwardly the person feels resentment, perhaps rage, against the presumed causes of the disease, near or remote, against present care, which is powerless to remove the apparent death sentence, and so on.

Bargaining is observed in the effort to make a deal with God, or with medical staff, or with the disease—to obtain more time.

Depression often replaces anger and bargaining as the probability of death is accepted. This may include feelings of remorse, unworthiness, and fear of death. Being able to experience and express this depression will help in moving beyond it, though it is likely to recur intermittently.

Acceptance may finally be reached, not as despair, but as detachment from people and things formerly valued, a quiet expectation of the step to come, however it may be conceived.

Dying persons should be allowed to accept the reality of their situation at their own pace. Information should neither be withheld from them nor thrust upon them. Ordinarily they will ask for it. Other people can help by making clear they are open to talk, by inviting conversation, and by responding honestly. Sharing of thoughts, questions, and feelings is a most important means for a person nearing death to make peace with the situation.

UNFINISHED BUSINESS

Dr. Kübler-Ross has pointed out the importance of encouraging and assisting dying people of any age to complete needed tasks and resolve relationships, including saying good-bye and making final arrangements and disposition of possessions. Identifying and completing this "unfinished business" helps bring an inner peace and acceptance of death. Frequently, a person facing death reflects on his or her life, seeking a sense of meaning and perspective. Dr. Robert Butler points out that what may seem to be garrulousness may be part of this "life review." Others can help by allowing time for listening, reflection, and sharing, perhaps taking down memoirs by hand or tape.[1]

Honesty among family and friends about the dying person's situation is needed to make possible this completing of tasks, and to avoid later regret about lost opportunities for communication.

Deciding about Home Care

Home care is not for everyone. Some families may not have the physical and emotional resources. More than half of people in nursing homes have mental deterioration making them especially difficult to care for at home,[2] and half have no significant family relationship.[3] A family with children at home may find the demands too great if one of the parents requires intensive care.

People have varying capacities to accept the demands home care makes of caregivers. It is important to recognize and acknowledge when limits have been reached, when the cost to other family members has become too great, and when resentment may erode the quality of care. Especially when a patient no longer recognizes the caregiver, the services received may be more important than who gives them. In addition, some patients prefer the security of institutional care in serious illness. Social workers in hospitals, health departments, and social service departments can suggest possible institutions.

Help for Home Care

If you decide on home care, a variety of resources are available. Local health departments and home health agencies are good places to start. If there is a local home-care hospice and the patient is eligible for its services, that will assist greatly. Explore the resources of family, friends, and religious organizations of which you are a member. Josefina Magno, first executive director of the National Hospice Organization, tells of a woman whose wish to die at home was realized because her synagogue organized help to assist with her care. There was no organized hospice at the time.

National sources for further information on home care are listed in Appendix 2, "Organizations." Associations for specific diseases can offer much pertinent advice. See Appendix 2, "Organizations." Be persistent in seeking what you need. Ask each source if they can suggest any other resource. Two very helpful books are *The 36-Hour Day: A Family Guide to Caring for Persons with Alzheimer's Disease, Related Dementing Illnesses, and Memory Loss in Later Life*, and *A Guide to Dying at Home*.

THE HOSPICE MOVEMENT

What is Hospice? Hospice is a comprehensive medically directed team-oriented program of care that seeks to treat and comfort terminally ill patients and their families at home or in a homelike setting, establishing pain management and symptom control as clinical goals, and understanding that psychological and spiritual pain are as significant as physical pain. Hospice is also a philosophy of care that accepts death as a natural part of life, seeking neither to hasten nor to prolong the dying process. In addition, hospice-style caring strives to help patients truly "live until they die"—without fear of dying in pain, dying alone, or losing control over how and where they will be cared for.

Hospice Services: These are available as needed, twenty-four hours a day, seven days a week. There are no holidays with hospice. Specific hospice services given to an individual patient are guided by a care plan. This plan is developed by an interdisciplinary team that includes a physician, a nurse, clergy, volunteers, and aides. More than ninety percent of hospice care hours are provided in patients' homes, thus substituting for more expensive hospitalizations.

Hospice services are often part of the covered benefits of Medicare, Medicaid (in forty-one states), and most private insurance plans. Some specifics of eligibility are given below in the section "More Facts About Hospice."

Besides direct care for the patient, hospice services include support for family members and friends while their loved one is dying, and bereavement care after the person has died. Most, but not all, hospices offer additional services to patients and their families, and to communities at large, such as memorial services, community educational programs on hospice care, individual and family bereavement counseling, and bereavement-education programs. (Sixty-nine percent of hospice patients and families accept bereavement services.)

More Facts About Hospice. There are more than 2,500 hospices in America; 97 of these have inpatient facilities. In recent years, the number has grown annually by nearly seventeen percent.

Hospices employ more than 25,000 paid professionals. At their side are 96,000 volunteers (mostly women) who, contribute more than five million hours of service per year.

In 1995, about 60 percent of hospice patients had cancer, 20 percent had Alzheimer's, 3 percent had AIDS, and 17 percent had other conditions.

Medicare coverage for hospice care is available if the patient is eligible for Medicare Part A, if the patient's doctor and hospital medical director certify that the patient is terminally ill with a life expectancy of six months or less, and if the patient signs a statement choosing hospice care instead of standard Medicare benefits for the terminal illness. And the hospice program must be one that is approved by Medicare.

Because of the rigorous standards for certification, many smaller hospices have not applied for certification and therefore are not eligible for Medicare payment. There is concern that as hospice becomes an institutionalized part of our health care system, it may tend to lose its former spirit of volunteerism, enthusiasm, and flexibility in meeting the needs of patients, families, and communities.

To Locate the Nearest Hospice: Contact your local health department or use the Hospice Help Line, 800-658-8898, or call Hospice Link 800-311-1620 (Monday through Friday, 9:00 A.M.–4:00 P.M. EST.)

Pain Control

Better ways of controlling pain in terminal illness have been a major contribution of the hospice movement. Using the same practices for chronic pain as are usual for acute care, as still often happens in hospitals, has led to a great deal of pain that could have been avoided. In hospice, chronic pain is controlled by giving sedatives on a regular basis, rather than waiting until the patient feels pain and asks for relief. This largely removes the fear and stress associated with chronic pain and may actually lessen the pain itself. Oral medicines are used rather than injections, which tend to become increasingly difficult. The key is careful combination of drugs and continuing precise adjustment of dosages as the condition of the patient changes.

Nutrition

Nutrition is another sensitive issue in terminal care. When the goal of patient care is recovery or prolongation of life, it is important for a patient to receive adequate nourishment. This in itself is difficult because seriously ill patients experience some loss of appetite. The patient will become less and less tolerant of food as his or her body deteriorates. When food is refused, caregivers often feel rejected or inadequate, being no longer able to offer this tangible comfort and fearing further decline of their loved one.

Hospice workers can offer help in maintaining good nutrition, and support and reassurance when this is no longer possible. In hospice care, as in hospital care, the question of artificial and/or forced feeding may arise. This raises complex questions for the patient, the family, and the hospice team, and no easy answers are available. Primary considerations should be respect for the wishes of the patient, and whether the benefits to be gained realistically outweigh the discomforts and cost. For further discussion, see Chapter 4, "The Right to Die."

A Caution

We rejoice at the growth of the hospice movement and the opportunity it brings to many for a humane and dignified death. As with any service, however, the increasing quality of care that accompanies professionalization is not without costs, both human and financial. We must take care to retain sensitivity and flexibility in home care, and to avoid unthinking acceptance of high costs just because we have grown accustomed to this in the acute-care cost structure of hospitals. Ideally, the hospice movement will help all health care institutions to become more responsive and flexible in meeting the needs of patients and their loved ones, and not to overwhelm the natural processes of life with complex technology.

Alzheimer's Disease

It is estimated that there are about four million persons with Alzheimer's disease in the United States in 2000, with no effective treatment or definitive diagnostic test available except at autopsy. It is the fourth leading cause of death among adults, with an as yet unknown origin. It produces progressive degeneration in the brain, called dementia, leading gradually to profound memory loss and eventually to complete helplessness. Some seventy-five percent of Alzheimer's patients are cared for at home, and are eligible for hospice care only in the final stages of the illness. The degenerative process lasts three to twenty years—eight to ten on the average—and caregivers usually experience many, often severe, stresses. Alzheimer's support groups are increasingly being formed, and excellent materials are available from the Alzheimer's Association, Inc. See Appendix 2, "Organizations."

Acquired Immunodeficiency Syndrome—AIDS

AIDS is a virus-caused disease first reported in 1981. According to the Centers for Disease Control, as of the beginning of 2000, the total number of reported cases in the U.S. was 733,374, of whom 430,411 had died.

The global epidemic has reached even more horrifying proportions elsewhere in the world. In June of 2000, the United Nations issued a report predicting that have of all 15-year-olds in South Africa and Zimbabwe may eventually die from the disease. Worldwide, the virus has killed 19 million people and infected 34 million more. While the crisis is most extreme in Africa, other parts of the world—including the Caribbean, Eastern Europe, and Asia—face catastrophe unless effective measures can be taken to slow the spread of AIDS.[4]

The virus breaks down the immune system, causing patients to be very susceptible to infections, especially the otherwise rare Kaposi's sarcoma (a cancer) and pneumocystis carini pneumonia.

Most adult patients with AIDS live at home, with occasional hospitalization for acute episodes of illness. Some special considerations apply to the home care of AIDS patients. The chance of a caretaker contracting AIDS is extremely low, since AIDS is spread primarily through sexual contact, use of contaminated IV needles, and blood transfusions. However, caution is advised. The Public Health Service recommends that caretakers wear gloves to avoid contact of skin and mucous membranes with blood and body fluids of AIDS patients, and surfaces soiled with blood should be cleaned with a household disinfectant.

Caution is recommended also to help a person with AIDS avoid exposure to infections. A most helpful book is *Living with AIDS—A Self-Care Manual*, edited by Lang, Spiegel, and Strigle, listed in Appendix 1, "Bibliography."

Obtaining appropriate health care and assistance from public and private agencies is sometimes difficult. The epidemic of anxiety concerning AIDS causes capricious and demoralizing discrimination. The discrimination against AIDS patients, however, is diminishing. Support groups and special advocates can help develop resources. There is no substitute for persistence in pursuing those services that are, or should be, available.

The National Hospice Organization adopted a policy in 1985 that calls on hospices to serve AIDS patients, and most programs are now open to people with AIDS.

Completing of unfinished business may be a special challenge and opportunity for those with AIDS. For men who contracted the disease through sexual contact with another man, openness with family, friends, and associates can present major difficulties. Near hysterical fear of the disease itself is sometimes compounded by a phobic reaction to homosexuality. Reactions of family members may range from acceptance to shock and outrage, complicated by embarrassment about irrational responses. While not all alienation can be resolved, many have found that facing death brings forth unexpected love and reconciliation, even when disagreements remain. Helpful organizations are listed in Appendix 2, "Organizations." Helpful books are available also.

The Dying Child

"All children know," Dr. Kübler-Ross says, "(not consciously, but intuitively) about the outcome of their illness. All little ones are aware (not on an intellectual, but on a spiritual level) if they are close to death." They are also aware of the pain and worries of their families and cannot be fooled about them. She counsels parents: "Tell them you are sad and sometimes feel so useless that you cannot help more. They will hold you in their little arms and feel good that they can help you by sharing comfort. Shared sorrow is much easier to bear than leaving them with feelings of guilt and fear that they are the cause of all your anxiety."[5]

While false cheer should be avoided, the family, and especially healthy children, should feel free to continue to laugh and play, bring friends home, and lead as normal a life as possible. "The worst thing we can do to the terminally ill child and the rest of the family is to make a morgue out of the house while the child is still living. Where there is laughter and joy, shared love, and little pleasures, the day-to-day difficulties are much easier to bear." Overprotection and overindulgence are to be avoided as confusing both to the sick child and to other children who are not similarly treated.

Brothers and sisters should be informed and "become part of the care in one way or another." At home, they can do tasks appropriate to their ages and even in the hospital they can make cheerful decorations or play favorite music on a tape recorder. "Such illnesses are much harder on the brothers and sisters than they are on the patient," Dr. Kübler-Ross comments. These siblings should have the support of a group or an adult to help them cope. They need special attention to their own situations and how they feel about what they are going through.

By continuing a normal family life as far as possible, and being sure that family members or friends spend extra time with healthy brothers and sisters, these children can share in the experience of caring, love, and grief without feeling neglected or wishing the child would die so that normal family life could be resumed.

Support for families with children who are dying is as essential as it is in situations where there is home care of an elderly person. Informal support structures or hospice organizations can offer strategic relief to the caregiving parent(s), and this is often overlooked. Call Children's Hospice International, 800-242-4453 (Mondays and Wednesday, 9–4).

General Comments on Dying

Kübler-Ross says, "Those who have the strength and the love to sit with a dying patient in the silence that goes beyond words will know that this moment is neither frightening nor painful. . . . Watching a peaceful death is like watching a falling star."[6]

"While death is easy, dying can be hard work," Deborah Duda adds.[7] Breathing may be labored or rasping, or quiet and spaced with long pauses. The person may grow colder and require additional covers, or may run a high fever and wish to shed coverings. Ice chips are good to relieve dryness of the mouth. There may be unusual or unpleasant odors. The patient may become somewhat disoriented or see hallucinations or visions. Most patients are comforted by the presence of a loved one, and many appreciate their hand being held. Persons who appear to be unconscious are sometimes aware of what is happening around them and what is being said. An elderly woman, apparently comatose, heard a nurse remark, "It's about time the old bitch died!" She later revived and mentioned the remark. It may be helpful to assure the dying person that those left behind will be all right, and that it is okay for him or her to let go and leave the body.

At death, as at birth, it is good to have someone present who has attended other deaths and knows what to expect. Hospice can be very helpful in this regard. Duda's book, quoted above, is specific and helpful. See the Bibliography at the end of this chapter. Caretakers and family members need to provide for their own needs, especially if the dying is prolonged.

An important advantage of death at home is that family and friends may sit with the body for a while. They may sit in silence, or talk to or about the patient, or pray. This time after death can be very helpful to survivors, in beginning to adjust to the loss. This is an old practice in some cultures, and some hospitals and nursing homes will cooperate, especially if it is prearranged.

It is my feeling that family members, especially children who are at hand when someone dies, should be encouraged to see the person who has died, but should not be urged. This may help them accept the reality of the death. After a peaceful death, cosmetic restoration, which makes the person appear lifelike, detracts from the experience.

When my first wife died, my daughter's two children were with me. I asked if they would care to see her before we put her body in the box. The girl said yes, the boy said no. That was all right on both counts. There was no cosmetic work and no public viewing. The whole thing was low-key and natural.

What is done next will depend on plans for the disposition of the body and for the memorial or funeral services. See Chapter 5, "Simple Burial and Cremation;" and Chapter 7, "Death Ceremonies."

ENDNOTES

[1]"Successful Aging and the Role of the Life Review," *Journal of the American Geriatrics Society*, 22:530, 1974.

[2]*Washington Post Health*, December 30, 1986, p. 13

[3]Robert N. Butler, M.D., "The Need for Quality Hospice Care," address to National Hospice Organization, 1978, p. 8.

[4]U.N. Joint Program on HIV/AIDS, June, 2000 Report. Additional statistics from National Center for HIV, STD and TB Prevention, Centers for Disease Control and Prevention.

[5]Quotations in this section are taken with permission from Elisabeth Kübler-Ross, *On Children and Death*. New York: Macmillan Publishing Co., 1983, pp. 1–3.

[6]Elisabeth Kübler-Ross, *On Death and Dying*. New York: Macmillan Publishing Co., 1969, p. 246.

[7]Deborah Duda, *Coming Home*. Santa Fe, New Mexico: Aurora Press, 1982, p. 219.

BIBLIOGRAPHY/CHAPTER 2

(Again, a few of many. For a wider selection, see Appendix 1.)

Coming Home, Deborah Duda. Aurora Press, 388 Calle Colina, Santa Fe, NM 87501, 1982. Practical and comprehensive handbook on financial, physical, emotional, and spiritual aspects of home care through serious illness and death. Highly recommended.

Gramp, Mark and Dan Jury. New York: Grossman Publishers (Viking Press), 1976, paper. A moving and honest account of the death at home of an eighty-two-year-old senile man, reported in word and photograph by his family, who honored his wishes and cared for him with love.

The Hospice Handbook, Larry Beresford. Boston: Little Brown & Co., 1993. Provides a complete account of the hospice movement with up-to-date information on current funding and care providing issues.

Living with Grief When Illness is Prolonged, Kenneth Doka. Bristol, PA: Taylor & Francis, 1900 Front Road, Suite 101, 19007.

Midwives To The Dying, Sherwood, OR: Angel's Work, 1992. Hospice nurses share their vast experience, compassion and skills related to how to help dying persons obtain emotional, physical, and spiritual comfort as they are dying.

3 BEREAVEMENT[1]

It is this sorrow of separation . . . this overspreading pain that deepens into loves and desires, into sufferings and joys in human homes; and this it is that ever melts and flows in songs through my poet's heart.

—Rabindranath Tagore

With every change we experience both gains and losses, and with the losses, grief, which is the process by which loss is healed. Some losses are small, passing almost unnoticed. Some are more serious—such as a divorce or the loss of a job or of a dream—and cause significant grief reactions. Some losses, such as the death of a loved one, are grievous. They cut us off from someone or something that gives life meaning, purpose, or security. With such a loss, we lose a crucial part of ourselves. It is as if we experience the death of those aspects of ourselves.

Grieving is the natural process by which a loss is healed. Understanding that there is a natural process to grieving can help us to feel more in control and to have more trust as we move through it. As we allow ourselves to experience grief, and if we can find the needed support, we will find ourselves with greater compassion, deepened and enriched relationships with others, and a more vivid sense of the meaning and value of life.

Cultural Barriers to Grieving

Grieving can be difficult in our culture, where grief and pain are often taboo. Necessary emotional support may be lacking if family and friends, uncomfortable with the pain, avoid the grieving person or the topic of the loss. Well-meaning people may encourage us to deny how deep the pain really is. Religious beliefs may be construed to suggest that the pain is unreal or should be quickly healed. Secular therapies also may gently pressure us to "integrate" the experience.

As we avoid facile comfort, we can also avoid unnecessary anxiety by understanding the grief process. We can know that we are not "going crazy," and that the devastating pain will not last forever, despite our feelings to the contrary. We will know how to help ourselves or others who grieve, and when special help is needed.

The Process of Grieving

Each person experiences loss in a unique way. At some time, however, most people will experience all of the following, some of them many times, and even after years have passed:
1. Denial, shock, numbness—protecting us from realization of the magnitude of the loss, especially in the case of sudden loss.
2. Emotional release—often a flood of tears, a realization of loss. This signals the beginning of healing.
3. Depression, loneliness, isolation.
4. Physical symptoms—some common sensations are: an emptiness or a hole in the pit of the stomach; a lump in the throat; tightness in the chest; sighing; a tiring or weakness of body; a lack of energy; dry mouth; headaches. A wide variety of minor or serious digestive, respiratory, hormonal, cardiovascular, and immunodeficiency symptoms are possible.
5. Panic—a person feels unable to cope with an unknown future, or feels there is something wrong with her or him.
6. Remorse—can range from an almost universal sense of one's shortcomings to the intense guilt often experienced either on the loss of a child or when there are unresolved conflicts or in the event of suicide.
7. Anger—at the deceased for dying, or at anyone who might be blamed for the death, or at God. Also anger at self, and guilt—for all the things "I should have done or said, or all the things I wish I hadn't done or said." This is normal, but may be difficult to face and share.
8. Need to talk—to express feelings, share memories, find meaning in the person's life.
9. Taking positive actions in response to a death—like working to avoid similar deaths for others, reaching out to persons similarly bereaved, completing projects of, or on behalf of, the deceased. This is always healing, but especially helpful for relief of guilt.
10. Readjustment—reaching out in new relationships and experiences.

My Own Experience with Grief

Again, I refer to my own family for experience in depth. When I was just a few months old my mother died, and my father and I went to live with his parents and with his older sister, who became my foster mother.

My father remarked once, late in life, "When someone you love dies, your love doesn't die, it gets redistributed." Profoundly bereft by the loss of my mother, he became a gentler, more caring person.

Much of his affection and of his hopes and dreams centered on me. I can't recall being punished or even scolded. Surrounded by loving adults I enjoyed an almost idyllic childhood. Discipline was no problem. I adored my father and was eager to do what he wanted. In a manner of speaking, my mother's death illuminated our lives.

Not until recent years did I realize that a warm and happy childhood has enhanced the sense of well-being that I've enjoyed throughout a long life. The death of a loved one—or just the awareness of the inevitability of death—can deepen our relationships and enrich our appreciation of the daily experience of living.

The experience of death took a very different turn when, in my teens, I lost, through cancer, the beloved aunt who had cared for me from infancy. Sadly bereft, I meditated deeply on life and decided that the best thing I could do for her was to carry on her life. Not necessarily her specific ideas, but the quality of her life, which was characterized by integrity and a profound human dedication. After that my grief went away.

During and after my first wife's death the bereavement was more profound. Together, over a period of forty years, we had homesteaded, raised a family, built a business, founded a school, and more. Together we had biked, canoed, camped, and climbed mountains. Without her my life was suddenly empty. I worked through this grief in several ways over a period of years.

For me, perhaps the most important form of release was in personal involvement. I helped take care of her before she died, helped lift her body into the box, and loaded it into my old station wagon. I drove to the burying ground, helped lower the box, and recited her favorite poem about death.

A day or so later we held a memorial meeting at the school, where I spoke for an hour and twenty minutes, telling of my wife's life. This did me a world of good. A few days later we held a meeting at Yellow Springs, Ohio, where we had lived most of our lives. Again I spoke, but this time for only forty minutes! Men, in our culture, have been denied ready access to tears, and speaking may provide emotional release instead. The importance of this often is overlooked because women usually outlive their husbands and we tend to assume that survivors are women.

While I was able to respond to the immediate challenge of my first wife's death, I knew that unless special measures were taken I would become ill once life returned to normal. So, as quickly as possible, I set forth on a business trip that would involve me in a tight schedule, associating closely with people. My health soon stabilized. I well remember my return from that trip. It was dusk, and as I drove down the mountain road toward home I thought sadly, "Elizabeth won't be there." The house was dark and I felt lonely. I phoned the school, which was nearby. "How about holding All-School Meeting at my house tonight?" I asked. Sure enough, a few minutes later students and staff arrived, filling the big music room, and a warm sense of fellowship came over me.

One aspect of bereavement that I had not anticipated was the loss of identity. With Elizabeth gone I was no longer me! After forty years of sharing such a broad spectrum of life, I did not have a separate identity. This was not painful, nor did it interfere with my activities, but it was very strange, and several years were required to get over it. I understand this is more often experienced by men, while women may feel a stronger sense of being deserted.

Happy involvement with many friends and ongoing projects soon restored to me a sense of well-being. It seemed that I had handled my bereavement well—and I had; but my wife kept appearing in my dreams. She wasn't dead after all—she had merely been away. It seemed so real that the happiness of her return would linger after I awoke. Clearly I still had a long way to go.

Some seven years after her death I found myself attracted to a young woman who embodied some of Elizabeth's qualities. I had no idea of marrying her because of the age difference, but the attraction continued. I finally realized that I was, in effect, projecting my wife onto her—trying in this way to bring back Elizabeth. With time and effort I was able to realize this and let go of my first wife. My attraction to the young woman then subsided to a cordial friendship. I was helped in this by being able to talk freely about it with my daughter, Jenifer.

Many years after Elizabeth's death, at age seventy-seven, I did marry again, very happily, a woman of my own age, whom I had known in college and who, like myself, had been widowed. We shared the same values and concerns. The marriage was a new one, not a reincarnation of the old one. In contemplating this marriage, I took serious pause at the problem of death. Did I really want to become vulnerable to death once more? During my marriage with Elizabeth there was always the shadow of a fear that I might die first, thus deserting her. With her death, this shadow vanished and I no longer feared death. Did I really want to become hostage to life again? Finally my new love and I made peace with death and agreed to a marriage that would be temporary—until one of us died. We deliberately accepted grief as part of life, and were thus free to enjoy our happiness.

Group Support in Bereavement

Group support is important for a family experiencing bereavement. See Appendix 2, "Organizations."

It was a beautiful Sunday morning in 1966. I was in Ohio, on the phone with my wife in North Carolina. Suddenly an operator broke in with an emergency call from Detroit. Our younger daughter, age twenty-nine, had been killed in a motor accident.

First I called back to my wife and broke the news to her. That was the hardest part. We set up plans for her to fly to Ohio. Then I phoned one of our friends, who was a member of the Friends Meeting (Quaker), asking him to get the word to the other meeting members. At 11:00 A.M. I went to meeting. Not much was said, but I could feel the love and support. I still remember the words of a thoughtful young man who spoke. "Until we have learned to accept death we are not really living." I found this a comforting thought.

Later I met my wife at the airport and brought her home. As if by magic meals appeared, chores were done, and errands were run. Old friends came to see us. Hospitality was arranged for relatives from out of town. A memorial meeting was quietly arranged. We seemed to be carried along on a gentle wave of love. We never learned who coordinated that—probably several people helped.* The memorial meeting was a heartwarming affair at which several people spoke, all spontaneously.

Looking back on that period, I am struck by the contrast with the occasion fifteen years earlier, when we experienced another death in the family. At that time the members of the meeting had been sympathetic, but there was no concerted move to give us the needed help. What had happened to change the situation so much for the better?

For one thing, the meeting had established a committee to organize help for families at a time of death. From this had grown the habit of doing that, to the point where it happened almost spontaneously. The fact that I turned to the meeting for help was probably important also. The habit of organizing immediate help for a family at a time of death is practiced in many religious groups. It is a good one to cultivate.

Another thing I would like to stress is the importance of visits by friends following a death. I recall an incident when my wife and I planned to visit a good friend whose husband had died but were a bit slow in getting to it. When we finally did, she met us at the door, exclaiming, "I *knew* you'd come!" The bereaved person normally has feelings of insecurity and often of guilt as well. The attention of friends is very important. Simple communication of the feeling of caring is probably the most important thing that can be done in the first hours or days after a loss. When the survivor feels like talking or expressing feelings, the listening and acceptance of a friend will help understanding and healing to emerge from within.

Children and Grief

Children, too, experience grief in a form depending on their age and circumstances. They need to accept the reality of loss and to mourn in their own way. Efforts to protect children from grief by explaining death as sleep or a journey can result in serious confusion. A child's questions should be answered honestly, in language he or she can understand. By the age of five children can

---

*Arrangements for immediate cremation were made through a quick call to the Detroit Memorial Society. Local affiliates of Funeral Consumers Alliance reciprocate in assisting one another's members. See Chapter 6, "Funeral Consumer Organizations."

begin to understand the permanence of death. It may be helpful to tell the child that the body of a dead person is peaceful and feels no pain, and that the child did not cause the death. The adult's feelings about the loss, and her or his religious beliefs, can also be shared in language understandable to the child. It is important to assure the child that she or he will be cared for and that they and those they love will be kept safe. As important as the words is the feeling behind them. The adult's degree of acceptance of death and faith in the future will be conveyed to the child.

The natural anger often expressed by children at the loss of a sibling, parent, grandparent, or friend may be shocking to adults. Earl Grollman's *Explaining Death to Children* gives useful guidelines for helping children deal with their anger, sadness, and guilt. See Appendix 1, "Bibliography." The pain and anger of a bereaved child may be expressed in nightmares, an inability to concentrate, moodiness, or in uncharacteristic roughness or violence. Children need an opportunity to acknowledge and express the complex feelings of bereavement. They can be helped, too, to understand the grief reactions of those around them. It is important that they be encouraged to feel free to continue enjoying their lives despite the loss that has occurred. Sometimes it helps for a family member or friend to explain to school personnel what is happening. See the Bibliography at the end of this chapter.

The Death of a Child

The grief experienced by parents when a child dies is particularly severe. Even when the dead child is an adult, loss of the hopes and dreams embodied in the child, and sudden inability to continue the caring and nurturing in which a parent's life is invested combine to prolong and intensify grief. The assistance of a support group or professional counselor often helps to meet these challenges, and to allow the parents to emerge from the tragedy strengthened and with a stronger relationship. It may be wise to begin such help as soon as the death is anticipated, even when there appears to be no grieving problem. To locate parent groups, see listings in Appendix 2, "Organizations."

When a child is lost, the relationship of parents is placed under special stress, too, because the normal support, reassurance, and intimacy of the relationship may also seem to be lost or threatened. The anger that is a normal part of grieving may be directed against a spouse. Each may experience the pain of seeing the other suffer and feel unable to help. And each will grieve in a different way, at a different pace. This can easily create tension and misunderstanding. The spouse, or other children, may remind a parent of the lost child, creating more pain within the family where one formerly turned for comfort.

It will help to realize that the couple relationship needs to be given priority, and to take time to listen, to share, to have fun together, to continue to touch and hug each other, and to renew other aspects of the relationship. Each needs to cultivate patience, to allow space in the relationship, and to realize that the spouse cannot be the only source of healing.

Once again, with understanding and time the loss can help illuminate their lives, helping them to become more loving and patient. I know a father who loved his children, but who was somewhat rough with them. Losing one through drowning, he suddenly realized what they meant to him and became kind and gentle. As a boy I lost a baby sister through sudden infant death syndrome. It was totally unexpected, and a great shock to us. Before the baby was taken away, my parents and I stood with our arms around each other—looking at the baby. That was a precious moment, filled with grief and love. The death of a child can draw a family together in warmth and tenderness.

The death of an infant before or shortly after birth is also an occasion for profound grief, complicated by the fact that society either may not recognize the loss or may regard it as a misfortune from which parents will quickly recover. Such a loss may happen suddenly and be a young family's first experience with death. They are likely to be unprepared for the strength and persistence of their grief. Family and friends may find it especially hard to recognize and accept the grief of fathers whose babies die.

Both parents should be encouraged to see the child, to name him or her, and to accept the reality of the child as a member of the family. It may help to have the hospital take the usual newborn photograph, and to save this along with the baby's hospital bracelet. Holding and being alone with the baby for a time may help. Not to recognize the existence and the loss of a child in such ways often results in parents' inability to accept the reality of the loss. This is reinforced by our general practice of acting as if an infant who dies has never existed.

The National Funeral Directors Association suggests that parents can be helped by "considering holding/dressing/casketing of the infant," as well as by "developing meaningful rites and rituals that involve the parents, grandparents, and siblings as participants and not mere observers."[2] Friends can help by acknowledging the event by words or caring gestures.

Loss of a child through abortion or adoption needs also to be mourned. Not only mothers, but fathers also frequently experience deep feelings of loss. Again, each must grieve the loss in his or her own way and time.

Suicide Survivors

Those bereaved by a suicide are often called "survivor victims" because of the intensified guilt, anger, and social stigma they experience. Healing includes the realization that the roots of suicide are complex and that no one, including parents and spouse, should be blamed. For a discussion of suicide prevention, see Chapter 4, "The Right to Die." See also Appendix 2, "Organizations," for a list of support groups.

AIDS Survivors

When someone with AIDS (acquired immunodeficiency syndrome) has died, bereavement is likely to have additional complications. Typically, those who die from AIDS are young, some in the midst of promising careers, with a whole future to be mourned. The intense fears and stigma often attached to the disease can make it extremely difficult for survivors to be open about their loss, greatly intensifying the loneliness and isolation typically felt by the bereaved. The support normally extended to the bereaved can be overwhelmed by negative attitudes, and practical arrangements are often greatly complicated. (See Chapter 5, "Simple Burial and Cremation," for help with funeral arrangements for AIDS victims.) Many resources that have been developed for AIDS patients and survivors are an outgrowth of the gay community and are less likely to serve others who are affected.

Special Issues for Bisexual or Homosexual Men

The family and friends of homosexual or bisexual AIDS patients may have to deal for the first time or in a new way with feelings concerning the person's lifestyle. Guilt and regrets for past decisions and attitudes may be intensified. Sadly, a surviving friend or lover may be excluded from funeral arrangements as family members assume the legal responsibility for disposition of the body, perhaps in violation of the expressed wishes of the one who has died. The loss may cause the survivor to lose his straight identity and to have to deal with resulting prejudice and discrimination. A surviving lover will face his own fears of contagion, and the normal resumption of social life will carry the added heavy burden of being a possible carrier of AIDS. Multiple losses may occur within one's social group, creating the feeling that one's whole community is a "sinking ship". Support groups exist in some urban areas, but many areas lack appropriate resources. Helpful written materials are available from the National AIDS Information Clearing House. See Appendix 2, "Organizations."

Other Situations of Bereavement

The impact of death touches others besides family and friends. In accidents or disasters, emergency workers need to give attention to their own emotional reactions as well as to the needs of the survivors. Those who cause the death of another are likely to feel intense guilt, which is itself a genuine and often devastating form of grief.

When my younger daughter was killed by a drinking driver, he wrote us a letter telling us how terrible he felt. This was helpful to us and, I imagine, also to him. Thinking about it afterward, it might have been helpful to have responded, acknowledging his grief in the situation.

When the *legal responsibility* for an accident is not clear, regret can be expressed in a way that neither accepts nor denies such responsibility. In these situations, as with the loss of a loved one, it is important to take time to be aware of the feelings and to accept feelings such as shock and grief, even when they are unexpected. Again, the best comfort one can offer is usually simply to be present and accepting, listening rather than telling, as the person experiences the varied aspects of grief.

Support Groups and Professional Help

Bereaved people often find peer support groups of great help in dealing constructively with their loss. Such groups exist for widows; parents who have lost newborns, infants, or older children; survivors of suicide and murder; and others. The National Self-Help Clearing House can help locate additional support groups, including groups for parents or patients with many diseases, injuries, or handicapping conditions. See Appendix 2, "Organizations." Books and pamphlets for the bereaved are available from these organizations.

Individuals or families wishing to locate the nearest support group—or to organize a support group—can also get strategic information from Support Works, the National Self-Help Clearing House (see Appendix 2, "Organizations").

A professional experienced in bereavement counseling can also provide healing assistance through the grief process. Acting as a guide, a professional can help the bereaved with unfinished business and saying good-bye.

Professional evaluation is indicated if a person experiences incapacitating depression, panic, unusual guilt, or excessive anger. Gradual or sudden onset of illness or weight gain or loss in excess of fifteen pounds is another sign that help may be needed. Prolonged lack of any feeling or continued denial of the loss also suggests need for professional assistance.

Good Physical Care

Research has demonstrated that grieving persons who take good physical care of themselves are more likely to avoid serious problems. This includes maintaining a balanced diet; paying attention to thirst and drinking adequate fluids to avoid dehydration (caffeine and alcohol act as diuretics and tend to increase dehydration); engaging in regular exercise; and resting when tired, rather than pushing to keep going.

Avoid the Use of Drugs

Tranquilizers are sometimes prescribed for persons in grief. These may be helpful as a temporary measure, but they numb feelings and tend to prevent the "grief work" that must be done. If medication becomes more than temporary, professional counseling should be sought.

Catastrophic Loss

Individual responses to loss can be multiplied in social upheavals to become powerful social and political forces. As an administrator of refugee relief in the Middle East in 1950, I was responsible for 25,000 homeless people. I became acutely aware of the grief they felt. The loss of home, country, livelihood, and sometimes of family members as well represented great bereavement. Many clung to denial, fantasizing a return to the homeland. There was a vast reservoir of bitterness and anger against those who were blamed. I believe that terrorism, nationalism, and warfare grow, in part, from these collective grief responses.

Along this line, many forces in our modern world create tragedy on a massive scale—shrinking forests; displaced cultures; expanding deserts; rising populations; millions of refugees from starvation, war, and genocide; vast poverty; and exploitation. Thus we find grief far beyond the normal—grief that must be dealt with at its roots. It is the responsibility of all of us to seek healing for this in whatever ways we can.

Bereavement Overload

It sometimes happens that the deaths of friends and loved ones are so numerous or so frequent that the individual hasn't the time or resources needed for healing. In such cases, we should reach out to one another and make the best of the situation.

How Death Illuminates Life

Death often has the effect of illuminating life. I have already told how my mother's death caused my father to become a warmer and more caring person and how this resulted, for me, in an almost idyllic childhood.

It can be helpful for survivors at a time of death to be aware of this potential and to draw strength and comfort from it. No one lives a full life without the experience of suffering. Whether we wither inside and are crippled by it, or reach out and grow with it, depends in large part on our understanding and our ability to let ourselves feel our pain and grow through our grief.

An important function of death ceremonies is to bring together the caring survivors—both family and friends—and strengthen the bonds among them. Also, to inspire a resurgence of the ideals and values that are meaningful to them.

It is a normal human trait to take for granted the family and friends who mean so much to us. The death of one of them can awaken us to the reality of what they mean to us.

This desirable result is helped by appropriate death ceremonies. My own preference is for a memorial service—held after the body has been removed—because attention then tends to focus on the life of the person who has died rather than on the dead body.

ENDNOTES

[1]We are especially indebted for help with this chapter to Donna O'Toole of the Compassion Books, and Alexis Stein, of To Life.

[2]National Funeral Directors Association, "Sudden Infant Death," 1981.

BIBLIOGRAPHY/CHAPTER 3
(A few of many. For a wider selection, see Appendix 1)

Aarvy Aardvark Finds Hope, Donna O'Toole. Compassion Books, 477 Hannah Branch Road, Burnsville, NC 28714, 1988. A charming read-aloud story for all ages about living and losing, friendship and hope.

Being A Widow, Lynn Caine. New York: Penguin Books, 1990. A well-written self-help book full of practical advice and words of wisdom written by someone who has been there.

Bereavement Magazine, 350 Gradle Drive, Carmel, IN 46032. Published nine times a year, this magazine is "a warm and caring friend that arrives in your mailbox." A helpful resource. Included with each issue is a substantial directory of support groups. An even more substantial directory may be had on request. Send a self-addressed stamped envelope—business size.) Subscription, $22 per year, $39 for two years.

Courage to Grieve, Judy Tatelbaum. New York: Harper & Row, 1980. A clearly written, insightful book on all aspects of the grief experience. Includes a practical self-help section.

Dying: A Book of Comfort, Pat McNees, Warner Books, 1998. A remarkable collection (331 pages) of quotations of comfort.

Grieving: How to Go On Living When Someone You Love Dies, Theresa A. Rando. Lexington, MA: D.C. Heath and Co., 1988.

Healing and Growing Through Grief, Donna O'Toole. Published by Blue Cross and Blue Shield of Michigan, 1986. Simple, clear, practical explanation of grief reactions and how to find your way through them to fuller life. Highly recommended.

Men and Grief, Carol Staudacher. Oakland, CA: New Harbinger Publ., 1991. A helpful guide for professionals and lay men and women about the effect of culture and gender issues on the grieving process.

4 THE RIGHT TO DIE

This chapter discusses the right of patients to refuse treatment, and the importance and methods of advance planning. It discusses suicide and suggests how to communicate effectively with potential suicides. It discusses the issue of assisted suicide, offers ground rules for self-termination, and speaks out against life-denying habits, which account for most self-destruction. It urges that compassion and common sense be used in making difficult decisions of principle.

The Right to Refuse Treatment

This matter has been given new urgency by the increasing availability of medical technology that, in the name of saving lives, commonly prolongs the process of dying, often at great cost in suffering and expense. At issue is the right and ability of a dying person to remain in charge of his or her body, choosing when to fight for life and when to be allowed to die. Now that eighty percent of the two million annual deaths in the United States occur in institutions, a whole team of professionals must often be persuaded to refrain from doing what they are trained to do.

Thousands of people are now being kept alive in permanently comatose condition with no prospect of recovery, and at a total cost of millions of dollars per year. Furthermore, as I commented in a previous chapter, some of these people, though totally unable to respond, may actually be aware of their circumstances and be leading a miserable existence.

The cost of futile death-prolonging treatment is often tremendous. An estimated forty percent of the average American's lifetime expense for medical care is spent in his or her last thirty days.[1]

The right to refuse treatment is based on the common-law right of self-determination and the constitutionally derived right of privacy. As long as the patient understands the nature and consequences of refusing treatment and can communicate those wishes, the patient's wishes control, even if doctors or family disagree. Violation of a patient's expressed decision can subject health care providers to civil damages. Patients who are competent do not lose this right upon becoming incompetent, provided they have indicated their wishes in writing and had them endorsed by their next of kin and family physician.

Families and physicians sometimes override a patient's wishes for a variety of reasons, although this violates the patient's legally protected rights. Families may be unable to accept the death of a loved one and let the person go, or they may be unwilling to risk the guilt due to failing to do everything possible for the dying person, or they may simply agree among themselves on what they see as a better course of action. More commonly a dying person did not indicate his or her wishes in the past and is unable to do so in the present. Medical personnel may act out of fear of legal liability, should any family member later question a decision to withhold or withdraw care.

Hospital personnel and procedures are focused on keeping people alive. To permit a death that could have been postponed may seem a failure, a violation of regulations, or unethical. Measures begun under pressure of an emergency become difficult for family and physician to discontinue. Under these circumstances, a patient who wishes to refuse treatment is too often regarded as unruly and is restrained or drugged to make him or her more tractable.

Discuss it in Advance!

It is of utmost importance to discuss these matters in advance and to record decisions in writing. This allows family members to anticipate and adjust themselves to possibilities in advance, and to make peace, even if not in total agreement with the dying person's wishes. As I said before, it means a great deal to a dying person if his or her family is able to accept the death. Similarly, if a person wishes to cut short a painful and costly dying process, the situation is eased by family acceptance of this decision.

Finances are a legitimate concern. Some people will choose not to exhaust their savings in expensive and painful efforts to prolong life for a brief period, when they feel these resources could be better used for the lives of their loved ones.

Important also is frank and ongoing discussion with the doctor concerning the patient's condition and prospects, and feelings concerning terminal care. Such openness should begin early, as it tends to become more difficult later on, especially for physicians under the intense pressures faced when providing critical care in a hospital. Most doctors appreciate the family's taking the initiative in this, as many find it difficult to do so and are unlikely to raise these questions.

If the ill or hospitalized person, or the family, feels at odds with the doctor after discussing the matter, it is proper to ask him or her to transfer the case to another doctor who will comply with the patient's wishes. If the doctor declines, ask the hospital administration to make the change. If they are unwilling, the matter may be taken to court to force the hospital either to honor the patient's wishes or to transfer him or her promptly to a complying physician.

Living Will and Power of Attorney

The miracles of medical technology are a tremendous blessing in saving human lives. But they can also prove to be a curse by prolonging the dying process at the cost of great suffering and expense.

It is important, while in good health, to formalize one's wishes in a Living Will, setting forth specific limits to treatment in the event of serious and irreversible illness. These are recognized by statutes in most states, and forms complying with each of these various laws are available from Choice in Dying. See Appendix 2, "Organizations."

Appendix 4, "Living Will," includes the standard living will declaration, along with an alternative living will, which my wife and I signed, and which goes somewhat further.

It is important that your living will be endorsed by your close relatives and by your doctor, and that it be witnessed by persons to whom you are not related by blood or marriage or who might in any way have an interest in your demise. Opposition to the living will is mainly based on the concern that relatives might seek to hasten a person's death for selfish reasons.

Artificial feeding remains a major issue. In some states it has been specifically exempted from living will directives, in compliance with the wishes of some right-to-life groups. Recent court decisions, however, have upheld the right of patients to refuse artificial feeding. If your state declaration does not clearly express your wishes, you may do so in an added statement on the form.

You should be as specific as possible about the type of treatment you especially do not want (for example, artificial feeding and fluids, antibiotics, chemotherapy, surgery, cardiac resuscitation). You should also be as specific as possible about the type of condition or quality of life in which you would not want to be artificially maintained (for example, permanent unconsciousness, severe dementia, end-stage AIDS with periods of lucidity).

The U.S. Supreme Court decision in the *Cruzan* case forbade the removal of the stomach tubes that kept the incurably comatose woman alive, on the grounds that, while she was quoted as having been opposed to such a procedure, she had left no written statement to that effect.

At the same time, the court broke new ground in affirming the right of a patient to refuse treatment, including food and water, and to leave written instructions to that effect.

So, if you dislike the idea of your dying being dragged out for weeks or months or years, record your wishes *now*, in writing, and be sure they are available in case they are needed.

If you wish to donate organs and tissues, a statement to this effect needs to be added to your declaration, authorizing necessary maintenance of the body until needed organs and tissues can be removed. Suggested wording is provided in Appendix 4, "Living Will."

Living will declarations should be backed up by a Durable Power of Attorney (DPA) authorizing a family member or friend to make health care decisions on your behalf should you be unable to do so. All states now make provision for such powers of attorney, and a few include this in their living will declarations. The making of health care decisions, including the authority to forgo life support, must be explicitly authorized. The updated forms for each state are available from the Hemlock Society or from Choice in Dying (addresses in Appendix 2, "Organizations"). It is not necessary to consult an attorney when completing these forms.

It is best to appoint the same proxy in all documents, and to specify a second proxy to act if the first one is not available when needed. The proxy may be a spouse, relative, or friend, although a few states limit who may be appointed. Bear in mind that this person may have to make difficult and painful decisions on your behalf. It is vital to discuss your treatment preferences with the proxy to make sure he or she understands your wishes and is willing to advocate on your behalf in an undoubtedly stressful situation.

It is important that copies of these documents be given to close relatives or friends, to any proxy you have appointed, and to your doctor. (Copies are valid.) Equally important, they should be included with your hospital chart if you are admitted to a hospital. If you change doctors, make sure your new doctor has a copy.

Support for the Right to Die

There is increasing support for the idea that the lives of terminally ill patients should not be prolonged by treatment against their will or the will of their family or designee if the patient is unable to decide. For instance, the American Medical Association's Council on Ethical and Judicial Affairs issued a statement on March 15, 1986, declaring that artificially supplied respiration, nutrition, and hydration may be withheld from a patient in an irreversible coma, even if death is not imminent. "In treating a terminally ill or irreversibly comatose patient," the council said, "the physician should determine whether the benefits of treatment outweigh its burdens."

As courts increasingly uphold the right to refuse treatment, a number of patients and their families around the country seek monetary damages from physicians and hospitals for not honoring a patient's rejection of treatment. The Hemlock Society's Patient Advisory Program will intervene for a member if an advance directive is being ignored or pain is not being treated.

The staff of Choice in Dying (see Appendix 2, "Organizations") can help in cases of conflict over withholding or removing life support. The staff draw on extensive knowledge of legal and institutional issues and can help callers resolve conflicts in the least adversarial manner. This free service is available to health care providers as well as to patients and their families.

Sensitivity Is Needed

While the principles may seem clear, many problems arise in carrying them out. It is not always clear when a condition is terminal or irreversible. Families and physicians need to be alert, too, to contradictory feelings in the patient who expresses a wish to be allowed to die. Temporary depression, unmet emotional needs, inadequate pain relief, and exaggerated fear of treatments sometimes enter in and should be considered before a decision is made.

The law is clear, however, that your wishes must be respected as long as you understand the nature of the treatment, the consequences of accepting or refusing it, and can communicate your decision. Other emotional, psychological, or intellectual problems are irrelevant as a matter of law.

It is important that sensitivity, compassion, and goodwill are exercised along with common sense, and that general rules are not rigidly applied.

The Dutch Example

Active euthanasia is practiced in Holland, where some 2,300 people a year die by requests for lethal injection, and about 400 more die by requesting a prescription for a lethal dose of medication that they self-administer. The practice is still not legal there, but no one is prosecuted for it if the rules have been followed.

The rules are very strict. Only the patient may ask for his or her death. No member of the family may ask for it, and the physician may not suggest it. Indeed the patient must ask for it several times, and the physician must agree that the request is a reasonable one. He must know the patient well and must consult with another physician before carrying out the request. The physician and the family members are routinely interrogated by the police.

In some ways the circumstances are more favorable in Holland than in some other countries. Everyone is guaranteed public health insurance, so the dread of financial disaster does not hang over the family as sometimes happens in America. Then, too, the relationship between doctor and patient in Holland tends to be somewhat closer and more long-lasting than here. Dutch culture, by and large, tends to be marked by gentleness and integrity. Some eighty percent of Dutch people favor the privilege of death on request.

Other countries, at first critical, are showing interest in the development and will no doubt follow suit in the course of time.

The Problem of Suicide[2]

The right to a merciful death for the terminally ill should not be confused with ending a life because of depression or failure to see other ways out of overwhelmingly painful circumstances. While the rate of suicide for all ages in the United States grew by 12.5 percent between 1957 and 1993, especially tragic was the 327 percent increase during the same period in suicides by people fifteen to twenty-four years of age.[3]

Each year nearly five thousand people under the age of twenty-four kill themselves in the United States, and experts assume that a significant number of deaths recorded as accidents are actually suicides. When one adds unsuccessful suicide attempts, 10 percent of students in high school and college may be at risk of suicide.[4] For ages fifteen to twenty-four, suicide is the third leading cause of death.

The transition from childhood to adulthood is an increasingly difficult period for many in our culture. Adolescents face many losses at a time when their accustomed sources of support may be weakest. Growing up means the loss of childhood—its innocence, freedoms, body image, relationships, and identity. The normal loosening of parental ties comes just as the young person is likely to meet intensified competition, hazing from peers, and loss of accustomed self-confidence. The relative security of the adult identity gained through such things as employment, marriage, children, and community involvement is not yet open to most teenagers in our high-tech, education-prolonging society.

With time and experience, most of us learn that even profound grief is not permanent, that eventually light will return to our lives. Adolescents often lack this perspective and are likely to have extreme reactions to loss, particularly because adolescence by its very nature is a time of extremes. Experiences such as a broken relationship, a family quarrel, academic failure, or derision from peers may seem like a final blow with no hope for a new beginning. For many, the possibility of nuclear catastrophe contributes to the difficulty in imagining a future for themselves. When life seems meaningless or overflowing with pain and stress, death may appear a logical choice. For the moment, the young person cannot see the irreplaceability of each human life, the fullness of life lived through and beyond pain, and the profound depth of suffering that such a death brings to others.

One vital challenge to modern education and family life, at least in the industrialized countries, is to involve young people in the work of the world in a meaningful way. Remembering how skillfully my parents did this for me, I realize in hindsight what it meant to my emotional well-being and sense of belonging.

Another key challenge, especially to educational institutions, is to cultivate among students a spirit of mutual affirmation and support rather than one of competition and put-downs. Success in this area can contribute enormously to a young person's feeling that life is really worthwhile. The Arthur Morgan

School, which originally published this Manual through Celo Press, stresses the importance of meeting these two challenges.

Help will come, too, from learning to handle grief at all stages of life, accepting it as a natural and inevitable part of being alive. In this way we can learn to help ourselves and others express and release their feelings, and thus transform the pain of losses into growth, rather than depression or despair.

While we try to do all that may be possible to reduce stresses and to provide supportive situations for young people generally, and those nearest us in particular, we can also seek to open our ears and our hearts to their thoughts and feelings. Especially we can be aware of danger signals, the "cry for help" that usually precedes suicidal actions. Take seriously expressions of despair, such as that life is hard and the future offers little hope, that one is weary of the struggle—no matter how unfounded others may feel these feelings to be. Inability to concentrate and recent excessive use of alcohol or drugs may be warning signs. Statements such as "death is peace" or "death is reunion" or "suicide is a reasonable alternative" are strong signals. Do not hesitate to seek professional help if such feelings persist despite supportive efforts of family and friends.

All of this can be very difficult to do. Parents' relationship with adolescents are likely to be strained. Real openness to the struggles of teenagers raises painful or unresolved issues for most adults, among them the handling of sexual feelings and relationships, dreams and disappointments in work and careers, acceptance or rejection by peers, academic and social competition, experiences of loss, and so on. The willingness to struggle and grow in one's own life is necessary if one is to accept and share the feelings of another without minimizing them ("it's really not so bad") or offering unhelpful advice or solutions ("just concentrate on your work and forget about him or her"). Studies suggest that when others accept the reality of a person's suicidal feelings, the chances of actual suicide are lessened.[5,6]

Focusing on the problem of suicide among young people should not cause us to lose sight of the need for much more attention to and understanding of self-destruction at any age. Suicide must be considered on a case-by-case basis if we are to truly learn its meaning and effectively develop ways to prevent it. Therefore, this discussion should be considered as only an introduction to a complex area of human life.

Ground Rules for Self-Termination

While strongly disapproving of suicide in most cases, I would point out that a rule intended to prevent one form of tragedy, if arbitrarily applied, may lead to other and worse forms of tragedy.

I hold that, for the terminally ill, the deliberate ending of one's life is sometimes a good and wise act. Since the word suicide carries overtones of tragedy and disgrace, it may be helpful to use a less judgmental word to apply to wise self-termination. I am concerned here with the difficult task of formulating principles to govern the decision for or against self-termination by those with drastic disability or incurable illness.

1. A decision to end one's life should *never* be carried out at a time of depression or despair. Likewise, pathological motives, such as a desire to hurt someone, should be guarded against.
2. Pain control should be double-checked. People are sometimes driven to suicide by chronic pain that can be relieved by change of treatment.
3. One's social role and relationships should be taken into account. Being a living burden on a loving family may be better than leaving, and may be less burdensome than the feelings experienced by the survivors following the commonly misunderstood act of "auto-euthanasia" (suicide). This is an individual and family matter. The conservation of social resources may be considered, too—energy, money, and medical resources.
4. The decision to end one's life should rest with the person in question, and the means for doing so should be in his or her hands.

Some Examples

An elderly doctor, learning that he had an incurable cancer, determined to enjoy fellowship with his family to the fullest during his remaining months of life and then, at the onset of his final decline and with their consent, to quietly end his life with an appropriate drug. Thus he would spare himself and them the pain and expense of going the hard way. The family agreed, and their last months together were deeply happy. His death did not involve suffering and his family, while they experienced grief and loneliness, did not suffer from shock or a sense of guilt.

Conversely, a doctor in my family, when asked by patients to help end their lives, would tell them which medicine, if taken all at once, would be lethal. The sense of empowerment that this gave to the patients, who no longer felt helpless, apparently helped restore the will to live. None of them took the medicine.

Similarly, I had a letter once from a woman I had never seen, who had a terminal illness and wished to cut it short. She said that none of her friends or family would talk with her about it, and asked if I would correspond with her—which I did. Exchanging letters, we discussed the pros and cons of ending her life and the various ramifications involved. I neither encouraged nor discouraged her. After a while she decided on religious grounds that she would rather stick it out and let nature take its course.

A Personal Message

The following letter was written by an elderly physician.[7]

To the Editor:

As one who has had a long, full, rich life of practice, service, and fulfillment; whose days are limited by a rapidly growing, highly malignant sarcoma of the peritoneum; whose hours, days, and nights are racked by intractable pain, discomfort, and insomnia; whose mind is often beclouded and disoriented by soporific drugs; and whose body is assaulted by needles and tubes that can have little effect on the prognosis, I urge medical, legal, religious, and social support for a program of voluntary euthanasia with dignity. Prolonging the life of such a patient is cruelty. It indicates a lack of sensitivity to the needs of a dying patient and is an admission of refusal to focus on a subject that the healthy cannot face. Attention from the first breath of life through the last breath is the doctor's work; the last breath is no less important than the first.

Consent by the patient, with a clear understanding of this act by the patient's immediate family, by the family physician, lawyer, minister, or friend, should violate no rules of social conduct. There is no reason for the erratic, painful course of the final events of life to be left to blind nature. Man chooses how to live; let him choose how to die. Let man choose when to depart, where, and under what circumstances. The harsh winds that blow over the terminus of life must be subdued.

Frederick Steen, M.D.
1240 West Park Avenue
Highland Park, IL 60036

Helping Someone to Die

A man I knew, in the final stages of cancer, asked his friends to bring him a drug with which he could end his life. This they did, but being very conscientious and wishing to be aboveboard, they notified the authorities about what they were doing. The sheriff's deputies rushed to the scene, but too late—the man was dead. No action was taken against the friends. Statistics gathered by the Hemlock Society indicate that this type of action is increasing.

Many cases of mercy killings have been reported. Compassionate doctors and family members undoubtedly do it more often than we know. One young man even honored his hospitalized mother's request to shoot her. A number of people have been brought to trial for such actions, but they usually pled guilty and received noncustodial punishment, with the exception of two cases recently, in which the accused received sentences of fifteen years and twenty-five years.[8]

Clearly it is the more dramatic type of mercy killing, such as shooting, that tends to call forth legal action rather than "gentler" procedures such as the administration of drugs.

A Legal Dilemma

Is it better to let assisted suicide remain outlawed, and then be humanely discriminating in enforcing the law, or to change the law itself? There is something to be said on both sides. Americans for Death with Dignity, for instance, proposes a national Humane and Dignified Death Act to legalize physicians' assistance to a patient in dying. The Hemlock Society (of which I am a member) provides counsel, information, and literature. A good discussion of legal considerations, "Euthanasia, Aiding Suicide and Cessation of Treatment," 1982, is available free by mail from the Law Reform Commission of Canada, 130 Albert Street, Ottawa, Ontario K1A 0L6.

Respectable Forms of Suicide

No thoughtful discussion of suicide is complete that does not make reference to people who kill themselves a little every day. While society deplores sudden suicide, it ordinarily condones the slow suicide implicit in a wide range of life-denying habits. Heart disease, for instance, our number one killer, can be greatly reduced by wholesome eating, appropriate exercise, avoiding overweight, and steering clear of tobacco. The second killer, lung cancer, in eighty-eight percent of cases is attributed to smoking. The third killer, automobile injuries (about fifty thousand deaths per year in the United States) can be cut more than half by the use of seat belts and by not drinking. Jellinek's disease (alcoholism) afflicts some twelve million people in the United States. It is said to shorten life by ten to twelve years and is involved in many auto accidents, eighty percent of home violence, thirty percent of suicides, sixty percent of child abuse, and sixty-five percent of drownings. Its economic cost is calculated at $54.1 billion annually. It is difficult to cope with because most sufferers firmly deny they have it.[9] The fourth killer, cirrhosis of the liver, is also associated with drinking.

The fifth killer, stroke, is commonly related to excess weight, as is hypertension, which is a frequent cause of stroke. Venereal disease is making a frightening comeback. The Centers for Disease Control reported a sharp increase in syphilis in the United States in 1980, and *The New York Times* reports gonorrhea as the most common bacterial disease of humans, with an estimated fifty million cases worldwide. Even more devastating is AIDS, which is assuming epidemic proportions and for which there is no known cure. All of these can be prevented.

The widespread excess consumption of sugar and caffeine also is conducive to degenerative disease. It is said that each of us consumes our weight in sugar annually. Heroin and other drugs claim thousands of lives and diminish the quality of life of thousands more. Increasingly, also, the pollution of our environment is taking a toll of life and health.

The "Study on Substance Abuse Toll," sponsored by the Robert Wood Johnson Foundation, found that the abuse of alcohol, tobacco, and drugs kills more than half a million people a year. The report by Brandeis University's Institute for Health Policy set the total economic cost of substance abuse on the U.S. economy at a staggering $238 billion in 1990.

In short, self-destruction is rampant in our society. Why do people indulge in life-denying habits and needlessly dangerous acts? Is it in part because they do not accept the reality of death? They think they are defying death, whereas they are actually denying it? It is commonly the person who has been most careless in his or her habits who, when the chips are down, clings most desperately to the shreds of life. Those who have lived fully and are at peace with their lives can most easily face death, including the choice of a time for its coming.

ENDNOTES

[1] *Yankee* magazine, "Man at the Crossroads," May 1984, p. 167.

[2] For help in understanding adolescent suicide we are indebted to Dr. John Schneider, *Finding My Way: Loss and Growth Across the Life Span*, unpublished manuscript, 1987.

[3] "Why 30,000 Americans will commit suicide this year," *U.S. News & World Report*, Vol. 96: April 2, 1984, p. 48.

[4] Michael Peck, "Youth Suicide," *Death Education*, 6:1, Spring 1982, p. 29.

[5] Jonelle Timlin, "Study Shows Most Counselors Favor Change in Euthanasia Laws," *Hemlock Quarterly*, Jan. 1983. Cites study showing that ignoring or rejecting someone's expressed desire to die is more likely to result in suicide.

[6] S. L. Dubovsky, "Averting Suicide in Terminally Ill Patients," *Psychosomatics*, Vol. 9, No. 2, 1978, pp. 113–5, showed decreased likelihood of suicide in patients allowed to openly discuss suicide.

[7] Quoted with permission from *New England Journal of Medicine*, Letters to the Editor, 303:15, Nov. 9, 1980, p. 891.

[8]Letter from Hemlock Society, March 3, 1987.

[9]*Newsweek*, October 17, 1983.

BIBLIOGRAPHY/CHAPTER 4
(See also Appendices 1 and 4.)

Death by Choice, Daniel C. Maguire. New York: Schocken Books, 1974, paper. Marquette University theologian wrestles with ethical questions of death by choice: deciding for yourself, deciding for others; legal killing (abortion, capital punishment, war). Highly recommended.

Ethical Decisions in Medicine, Howard Brodie. Boston: Little, Brown & Co., 1976. Examines issues of informed consent, quality of life, ethical participation, allocation of scarce resources, and euthanasia. Highly recommended.

The Euthanasia Review, quarterly. Human Sciences Press, Inc., 72 Fifth Ave., New York, NY 10011-8004; 212-243-6000.

Final Choices: To Live or to Die, George Burnell. New York, NY, Insight Books, 1993. This book is to prepare lay people to face the difficult task of preparing for their own impending death in an age of medical technology.

Final Exit, 2nd ed., Derek Humphry. New York, NY: Dell, 1992. An up-to-date guide to the do's and don'ts of self-delivery for terminally ill patients.

Final Passages—Positive Choices for the Dying and Their Loved Ones, J. Ahronheim and D. Weber. New York: Simon & Schuster, 1992. This book provides answers to the questions faced by seriously ill and dying persons and their families. Provides information on many alternatives.

Medicide: The Goodness of Planned Death, Jack Kevorkian. Buffalo, NY: Prometheus Books, 1991. The author shares his controversial views on the need to have U.S. physicians assist individuals suffering painful or debilitating illnesses to die peacefully.

And more titles, which may be ordered from The Hemlock Society USA, P.O. Box 101810, Denver, CO 80250-1810; 800-247-7421:

A Midwife Through the Dying Process, Timothy Quill. Baltimore, MD: Johns Hopkins Press, 1997.

How We Die, Sherwin Nuland. New York: Random House, 1996. A surgeon tells the clinical details of the various causes of death and how they happen.

The Good Death, Marilyn Webb. New York: Bantam Doubleday Dell, 1998. A journalist examines the dying of different people and thoroughly discusses all options.

Assisted Suicide, Stephen Jamison. San Francisco, CA: Jossey-Bass, 1998. This decision-making guide for health professionals explores all the meanings in a request for a hastened death.

5 SIMPLE BURIAL AND CREMATION

This chapter discusses funeral costs and how to control them; how to get dignity, simplicity, and economy in funeral arrangements; the options for body disposal; the values of simplicity; and the importance and methods of planning. It also discusses financial planning, including prepayment plans, outlines things to be done at the time of death, and tells about funerals conducted without funeral directors.

For help in preparing this chapter I am indebted to Harvey Lapin, general counsel to the Cremation Association of North America and the National Funeral Directors Association; the Funeral Consumers Alliance (FCA); Howard Raether, former executive director of the National Funeral Directors Association; and Rev. Henry Wasielewski, of the Coalition for Fair Funeral Prices.

Despite soaring funeral costs nationally, it need not always be expensive to arrange for burial, cremation, or donation of a body.

In Celo Community, for instance, where I live, the complete cost of burial in our community cemetery is about twenty-five dollars. This is made possible by a committee of our Quaker meeting, which provides moral and practical support to families at times of death. In addition to assisting with meals, child care, hospitality, and the necessary paperwork, the committee quickly puts together a simple plywood box, digs a grave, and handles the burial. Family and close friends who wish to may view the body before burial, without cosmetic preparation. Later a memorial service is held focusing on the life and personality of the one who has died and on the spiritual aspect of the occasion.

Throughout the United States there is a scattering of groups and families, most often in rural areas, who care for their own dead without professional help. Some are coordinated by religious organizations, others by families or communities. "Nonprofessional Funerals," later in this chapter, describes this in more detail. Chapter 7, "Death Ceremonies," gives complete instructions for organizing a memorial service.

In Canada there is a growing movement of cooperative mortuaries, mainly church-led but not usually confined to church members. There are a few in the United States as well.

Many groups and individuals obtain reasonable prices for burial, cremation, and/or funeral services through careful shopping and negotiation before a death occurs. Funeral consumer organizations (formerly known as Memorial societies), described in Chapter 6, do this in over 150 communities in North

America. Other ways of doing this are described in "Planning without a Society" and "Simplicity Without Preplanning" in this chapter.

Despite these options, the commercialization of funeral rites in Canada and the United States has resulted in expensive and often ostentatious funerals, at costs rising almost twice as fast as the cost of living. An estimated eight billion dollars is spent on funerals in the United States each year, not counting cemetery costs. According to the National Funeral Directors Association the average cost of an adult funeral in the United States, with all the trimmings, is about $4,800. To this must be added the average cemetery charge of $1,200 or more, bringing the total cost for body disposition to around $6,000, the largest single purchase, after a house and car, for many families.

It is only fair to mention that there is a sprinkling—and growing number—of maverick funeral directors who thoughtfully assist their clients in getting economy, and are able to operate solvently in the process.

We heartily agree with funeral directors that death ceremonies, wisely planned, are important in meeting the social and emotional needs of survivors. See Chapter 7, "Death Ceremonies." We would add, however, that the amount of money spent has little to do with how well they meet those needs. Families who want to, and can, pay for expensive services should certainly have them, but there are alternatives that are much less expensive and can meet the needs as well or better.

Why Are Most Funerals So Costly?

Funeral directing is honorable and necessary, but is in a unique situation. About 22,000 funeral homes in the United States handle about two million deaths per year, about ninety-five each. However, a tiny fraction of the funeral homes handle a majority of the business; thus many have less than one funeral per week. How do the thousands of morticians survive whose businesses are idle more than eighty percent of the time?

Some have other sources of income. In the old days the undertaker usually ran a furniture store, and conducting funerals was a sideline related to the sale of merchandise he carried. Today, however, funeral directors who average as low as one funeral a week and have no other business must charge the overhead of days and weeks of idleness to a single funeral. Only by charging exorbitant prices can these businesses survive. Such prices are possible because competition does not exist in this business in the same way it does in others.

Mark Twain puts it neatly in *Life on the Mississippi* with an undertaker saying:

> There's one thing in this world which a person don't say—"I'll look around a little and if I can't do better I'll come back and take it." That's

a coffin. And take your poor man, and if you work him right he'll bust himself on a single layout. Or especially a woman.

Most bereaved relatives, in a state of shock and grief following a death, see no alternative to accepting what a funeral director presents as proper and acceptable. The funeral directors, in turn, are naturally concerned as business people to sell sufficient services to meet expenses. This in itself is not illegal or unethical, but creates a serious problem for consumers.

Another important factor is that a substantial portion of the funeral industry—especially the larger firms—has been taken over by large chains who also operate many crematories, cemeteries, and flower shops.

Regulation of the Funeral Industry

This situation in the funeral industry has naturally led to abuses, and these were dramatically brought to public attention in 1963 by Jessica Mitford's *The American Way of Death*. Even in 2000 the U.S. Senate Committee on Aging rated these abuses among the most harmful frauds directed against the elderly.

In the United States, the federal and state governments and the funeral industry itself have taken steps to curb these abuses and improve industry practices. The Federal Trade Commission, after years of study, public hearings, and legal appeals by industry groups, approved a consumer protection rule requiring itemized price disclosures by funeral directors before arrangements are made, including price disclosure by telephone. Funeral directors, however, are not required to notify phone callers that prices are available over the phone.

Funeral directors are forbidden to charge a casket-handling fee if someone brings in a casket that he has made or has purchased elsewhere.

Misrepresentations and unfair practices that were once common are legally forbidden. Surveys by local funeral consumer organizations and others, however, have found extensive noncompliance with these rules.

Individual states have additional consumer protection laws, but there is often confusion about these laws. Some funeral industry practices are required by law, some are not. Funeral directors are not always sure which are which and sometimes give incorrect information to clients. As one member of a regulatory board remarked, "Funeral directors are a gold mine of legal misinformation."

Laws regulating the funeral industry are based on the state's right to protect public health and safety. In many states, however, laws and regulations appear to have been drawn more in the interests of the funeral profession than of the public. For instance, while a few states require embalming when a person has died from a contagious disease, the prevailing medical opinion is that no public health purpose is served by embalming.

It has been suggested that a "Truth in Death Services Act" would be helpful. This would be similar to the Truth in Lending and Truth in Packaging acts.

Funeral directors, like other business groups, have active lobbies in most state and provincial capitals. Most of the boards that regulate the funeral industry are composed of funeral directors. Regulations made by these boards acquire the force of law. Such regulations usually pertain more to such areas as qualifications of funeral directors and funeral home requirements than to consumer issues.

Consumer groups advocate that such regulatory bodies should instead contain a majority of nonindustry members and provide full representation of the consumer viewpoint. It is important that funeral consumer organizations and other consumer groups be alert to legislation affecting funeral practices and vigorously defend consumer interests. Consultation in such legislative efforts is available from the Funeral Consumers Alliance (FCA). See Appendix 6, "Directory of Funeral Consumer Organizations."

Where to Go with Complaints

The best place to start with funeral complaints is with your local funeral information organization or the national umbrella group, Funeral Consumers Alliance (FCA). Call 800-765-0107. They have on file all the laws for every state, as well as the Federal Trade Commission's (FTC) Funeral Rule. FCA also offers free service on the Internet—to check their funeral law library—and can answer many questions. Their information-packed Web site is located at http://www.funerals.org. FCA makes the following statement:

> Sometimes we have to educate folks about what is reasonable or legal. Otherwise, we generally recommend that funeral complaints get filed with a funeral board (except in Colorado, where there isn't any)—with a copy to the consumer protection division of the state's attorney general's office. (We have all such addresses in this office, too.) Sometimes we have to help folks in wording the complaint to fit the part of the law or regulation offended. "It was a bad funeral" isn't good enough, so we coach people on how to phrase their complaint to be relevant to the statutes. Many times, a copy should be filed with the regional FTC office. And we ask for a copy here in this office.

Complaints about funeral directors may also be submitted to the Funeral Service Consumer Assistance Program carried on by the National Research and Information Center. Complaints concerning cemeteries may be referred to the Cemetery Consumer Service Council. Complaints about burial monuments can be sent to Monument Builders of North America. See Appendix 2, "Organizations," for addresses and and phone numbers.

Keep in mind that these organizations, while frequently helpful, are operated by their respective industries and are as much concerned with the industry as with the consumer.

A major source of information and assistance, of course, is the Funeral Rule office of the Federal Trade Commission.

If a funeral director is unwilling to submit a complaint to binding arbitration, the consumer may address the state licensing board (c/o the governor, if the address is not known), sending copies to the state attorney general's office and to appropriate consumer protection agencies at the local, state, and national levels.

The Funeral Consumers Alliance has a legal fund for class-action type situations or where laws and regulations are not clear.

AIDS and Funeral Directors

Consumer organizations have received many complaints about funeral homes refusing to handle bodies of persons who have died from acquired immunodeficiency syndrome (AIDS), or pressuring survivors who request burial to use cremation instead. In California and New York, advocacy groups have conducted surveys to identify funeral directors who will serve AIDS victims, and health departments and human rights agencies have checked on discriminatory practices by funeral directors. Airlines have also refused to transport bodies of AIDS victims, although normal requirements preclude any hazard. Health departments and the National Funeral Directors Association advise that bodies of AIDS victims may be safely handled using the precautions normally taken for the more contagious hepatitis B virus.

What Are the Options for Body Disposition?

The following options are listed in approximate order of cost, with the least expensive first. There is a great deal of variety within most of these options, which will be discussed later.

1. Immediate removal to a medical school, followed by a memorial service. If, at time of death, a body is accepted by a medical school, this generally involves no cost and performs a valuable service. Alternative plans should be made in case the body is not accepted. If you plan to leave your body to a medical school, it is wise to sign the necessary papers years in advance. This ensures the acceptance of your body even though no new bequeathals are being accepted. Many schools require the family to pay transportation. A few require arterial embalming at family expense. See Appendix 8, "Anatomical Gifts," for addresses and instructions on donations and

alternate plans. There can be a brief gathering of the family before removal if circumstances permit, but this must be done quickly. See Chapter 7, "Death Ceremonies."

2. Immediate burial without professional help. This may be done by the family, a religious group, or a community group. It can be followed by a memorial service. See "Nonprofessional Funerals," page 62.

3. Immediate cremation, followed by a memorial service. Removal to the crematory can be handled by a funeral director or by family or friends. There may also be a committal service at the crematory chapel if desired, and/or later with the disposition of the ashes. See page 61, "About Cremation" and "Disposition of Cremated Remains." Sample ceremonies are provided in Appendix 7, "Death Ceremonies."

4. Immediate burial handled by a funeral director, followed by a memorial service if desired. There may also be a graveside committal service if desired. Embalming is not required.

5. A funeral service in the presence of the body, followed by cremation or donation to a medical school. In this case embalming is usually chosen.

6. A funeral service in the presence of the body, followed by earth burial.

What's the Difference Between Funeral and Memorial Services?

A funeral service is, by definition, a service held in the presence of the body. The casket may be open or closed. A memorial service is a service held after the body has been removed. Both serve the same purpose. Each has something to recommend it. A discussion of the two types of services will be found in Chapter 7, "Death Ceremonies."

The Practice of Simplicity

Simplicity in arrangements can effect great economy, but even more importantly it can help center attention on spiritual values and the life of the person who has died, rather than on material things. It can avoid the appearance of ostentation and extravagance. Removal of the body within twenty-four hours, followed by a memorial service, allows the ceremony to focus on the life of the one who has died, with the healing that can bring.

Family Participation

Family members can be helped to recognize and accept a death and to begin the process of grieving by helping in the removal and disposition of the body. It is often good for the closest family members to be given an opportunity to accompany the body to its destination and to help load and unload it. If burial is used, they may accompany the body to the graveside and start the filling of the grave. Family or friends may have a suitable vehicle, such as a station wagon, van, or pickup truck, for conveying the body, and a family member should be encouraged to drive it. A hearse is not required. The length of the box for transporting a body should be considered in choosing a vehicle for transportation.

There may be a brief committal service at the graveside or crematory. This may include a prayer, poem, or song, as desired. Chapter 7, "Death Ceremonies," contains many suggestions for meaningful participation in funerals and memorial services by family and friends.

The Need for Planning

Simplicity doesn't happen by accident. When death occurs in a family in which there was no planning, the survivors find themselves virtually helpless in the face of entrenched custom, dealing with a funeral director who expects them to follow this custom. Through planning, however, family members can have the precedent, information, and moral support needed to get the type of service they want.

Thousands of Families Being Helped

To help with advance planning, nonprofit funeral consumer organizations have been formed in some 150 cities in the United States and Canada with a membership of nearly a million. These societies cooperate with funeral directors, sometimes by having contracts with them and sometimes by advising their members as to which firms provide the desired services. They also assist those who wish to leave their bodies for education or their eyes or other tissues for transplant or therapy. See Chapter 6, "Funeral Consumer Organizations."

Friends of FCA

For those who do not have ready access to a local or regional funeral consumer organization there is a national society, which anyone can join. It is Friends of FCA and is sponsored by the Funeral Consumers Alliance (FCA), P.O. Box 10, Hinesburg, VT 05461; 802-482-3437.

The enrollment fee is twenty-five dollars, which includes the first year's dues. This entitles the member to receive a kit of books and documents valued at over fifty dollars, giving comprehensive information and instructions on problems relating to death, plus newsletters and special bulletins throughout the year.

Membership in Friends of FCA entitles the member to join any local or regional funeral consumer organization without additional charge, and to call upon any nearby chapter for help—also without charge.

In some areas, where there is no local chapter, FCA has located a low-cost mortuary and is monitoring consumer satisfaction with those who have used it. More detailed information about Friends of FCA can be had on request from FCA.

Also available from FCA, for one dollar, is an up-to-date directory of local funeral consumer organizations. Some of the local chapters have connections with, or information on, funeral directors over a considerable area. Much depends on the kind of services wanted. It may be economical to use a funeral director or a crematory quite far away if the body needs to be transported only one way, as when a memorial service is used instead of a funeral service in the presence of the body.

Planning Without a Local Consumer Organization

The simple arrangements and low rates obtained through a funeral consumer organization may sometimes be obtained by individual arrangement, though this is likely to be difficult. Sometimes a church or a labor or fraternal group can find a cooperative funeral director and make such arrangements on behalf of its members. In such cases it is good to keep participation open to nonmembers and to look forward to becoming a full-fledged funeral consumer organization.

The family should talk the matter over, preferably while all are in good health, and decide whether cremation, burial, or donation of the body to a medical school is preferred, whether there shall be viewing of the remains, and whether a funeral or memorial service is wanted. These are the main decisions. Then call or visit various funeral directors, explaining your wishes, and see what each has to offer.

Local Surveys of Funeral Costs

In several places, the local newspaper or broadcasting station has made a survey of funeral costs. These have produced phenomenal public response.

Sometimes these surveys are made by the newspaper or broadcasting station itself and sometimes they are made in cooperation with the Better Business Bureau or with a funeral consumer organization, a civic or senior citizen organization, a church, or a group of churches.

For suggestions on how to conduct such a survey, or for printed forms to use in conducting a survey, contact the National Coalition, or the Funeral Consumers Alliance (See Appendices 2 and 6). They can supply excellent material, including videotapes for television use.

Planning Helps Understanding

Advance planning is needed, not only in making arrangements with funeral directors, but for working out understanding within the family. A young man killed in an accident left a widow and young children with no savings. Both husband and wife believed in simple burial, and the widow was fortunate in getting a funeral director who encouraged her to carry out her desire for a simple and economical arrangement. The young man's mother, however, though unable to help with the expenses, insisted on an elaborate funeral. Since there had been no advance planning, the wife was unable to resist and not only had to endure a ceremony distressing to her, but had to face life with small children, her husband gone, and a heavy funeral debt hanging over her. More explicit planning might have avoided this unhappy outcome.

Persons wishing to leave organs or tissues to aid the living, or who wish to leave their bodies to a medical school, have a particular responsibility to reach an understanding with their families ahead of time.

If a family is not in agreement about body disposition, the surviving spouse, or other survivor if there is no spouse, has the legal right to make the decision in most states. A lawyer should be consulted if a person wishes to make plans or arrangements binding on survivors.

Write it Down!

A valuable help in planning is a four-page form called "Putting My House in Order," which is available from the Funeral Consumers Alliance. See Appendix 6, "Directory of Funeral Consumer Information Societies." Plans for body disposition and death ceremonies, as well as financial and property records, can be indicated on this form. Similar though less detailed forms are available from the NFDA and several cemetery associations. See Appendix 2, "Organizations." Do *not* include funeral plans in your will, as wills are seldom read until after the funeral.

Simplicity Without Preplanning

If you desire simplicity and economy but are confronted with a death in the family without advance plans, there are still alternatives, though not as easy. First of all, consider the options listed on page 52 of this chapter.

If you opt for immediate removal to a medical school, consult the Directory of Medical Schools in Appendix 8 to determine which, if any, medical schools within a reasonable radius are in need of bodies, then phone the anatomy department there to see if the body may be accepted.

If you prefer some other alternative, check to see if there is a funeral consumer organization in your area. See Appendix 6, "Directory of Funeral Consumer Organizations." Call the chapter in your area. It may be too late to join, but, in any case, the volunteer will give you as much advice, moral support, and information as possible. Many chapters will accept members at this time.

If this can't be arranged, ask some knowledgeable friend, perhaps your clergyman, to help you locate a cooperative funeral director. The 1984 Federal Trade Commission (FTC) rule requires funeral directors to provide price information over the phone on request, as well as in person. *Be sure* your friend goes with you to see the funeral director and help make arrangements. Your friend can ask questions without embarrassment and can give important moral support.

Bear in mind that funeral directors are often skilled merchandisers who downplay their cheaper merchandise. Don't be put off if the funeral director refers to a simple service as a "welfare funeral." An itemized price list of services and merchandise must be presented, whether requested or not, before arrangements are made, under the FTC rule. While funeral "packages" are still offered, you are no longer required to accept this, and items deleted must be deducted from the costs charged.

If you prefer to make your own burial box, find a funeral director who is willing to handle this, rather than selling his or her own merchandise. As mentioned elsewhere, a funeral director cannot legally charge a casket-handling fee in such cases. Some funeral directors will rent caskets, if viewing is desired but will be followed by cremation rather than burial. The key is shopping around, preferably in advance.

FINANCIAL RESOURCES AT TIME OF DEATH

Social Security Death Benefits. A Social Security lump sum death payment of $255 is available in some cases to survivors of covered workers. This benefit must be formally applied for. Those eligible are:

1. A surviving spouse living with the covered worker at time of death. This includes a spouse separated *solely* for medical reasons, such as residence in a hospital or nursing home.
2. A surviving spouse *not* living with the covered worker at the time of death is eligible for the payment only if she or he was receiving a monthly benefit as a spouse during the month of death or would have been eligible for such benefit if an application had been filed for it.
3. If there is no surviving eligible spouse, a child will be eligible for the lump sum payment if he or she was eligible for Social Security monthly benefits on the deceased's record during the month of death of the covered worker.

Union and Fraternal Benefits are provided by many trade union and fraternal organizations to the families of their members. Many such benefits go unclaimed because families are unaware of them. Also, there are benefits for the survivors of any man who has ever been a railroad employee. Some of these benefits are available only for funeral expenses.

Insurance and Employee Benefits. No family needs to be told to file claims for life insurance. Often, however, there are other forms of insurance, depending on the circumstances of the death, which provide benefits for the survivors. If occupational factors were involved in the death, Workman's Compensation Insurance may be in effect. There may be automobile club insurance. In other cases liability insurance of one kind or another may be invoked. The families of state employees in some states are entitled to survivor benefits. Such possibilities should be checked. Burial expenses for indigent families are commonly paid by the county.

Benefits for Veterans and Their Dependents are substantial, but are very complex, depending on a variety of circumstances. They are supplied by the Veterans Administration. FCA can supply a six-page folder entitled "Veterans' Funeral and Burial Benefits," which contains detailed information. Don't rely entirely on your funeral director for this information.

Families of veterans also may be eligible for ongoing financial assistance in the form of monthly survivor benefits. Your local Social Security and Veterans Administration offices and your funeral director can assist you in obtaining these benefits. Be prepared for a lengthy process. For detailed information send for VA pamphlet 27-82-2, from Department of Veterans Affairs, Washington, DC 20420.

To reach the regional Veterans office in your area, call 800- 827-1000.

Protection through a Credit Union. One of the best and most economical ways to provide for funeral expenses is through a credit union.

There are thousands of credit unions in the United States and many of them offer one or more insurance arrangements for their members. The arrangements are called Life Savings Insurance.

There are several arrangements, varying with the age of the depositor and the timing and size of the deposit.

A description of the plans is too long to include here, but can be had from your local credit union or by addressing the Credit Union National Association (CUNA) at 5910 Mineral Point Road, Madison, WI 53701; 800-937-2644.

Life Insurance. Many families carry a small insurance policy on each member for the specific purpose of meeting burial expense in case of death. In such cases, the family should decide in advance what types of services are wanted and what they are likely to cost. Otherwise the expense may be several times the anticipated amount. Just as inflation makes life insurance a poor form of savings, so it makes it a costly way to provide for death expenses—though better than none.

Mutual Aid Plans. Some groups, including a number of Mennonite Church congregations, assess each family when a death occurs.

A Totten Trust is a savings account in your name to which is added "in trust for . . ." (the relative or friend who is to use the funds as you direct). It may be in a credit union, bank, or other savings institution. Be sure to check the interest rate, however, as it may be relatively low.

Prepaid Funeral Arrangements

Much promotion has recently gone into the selling of prepaid funeral contracts. A million or more are being sold each year at a cost of billions of dollars. All too often the selling of these arrangements provides an occasion for "upgrading" the funeral (making it more expensive).

In general, a consumer can get the same security and benefits by placing the funds in a savings account or trust for funeral purposes, a credit union, or other conservative investment. Such funds remain under the control of the consumer and can be transferred to another location or institution without penalty. They can be changed, if desired, or withdrawn, complete with accumulated interest.

Although most states have some type of legislation governing pre-need sales, the laws in some states have not been adequate to prevent a significant increase in complaints from consumers, like allegations of deceptive marketing or of difficulty in obtaining refunds when moving or canceling a contract. In response, the American Association of Retired Persons, the organization now known as Funeral Consumers Alliance, and Consumer Federation of America in 1987 prepared "A Model Law for Prepaid Funeral Arrangements," incorporating necessary consumer protections.

The issue of prepaid funerals is a big problem in almost every state. Lisa Carlson devotes a whole chapter, "The Body Snatchers—Pre-need Greed," to this matter in her book *Caring for the Dead—Your Final Act of Love* (available from FCA).

Another resource on this topic is a booklet published by the Consumer Affairs Program department of the American Association of Retired Persons (AARP), at 1909 K Street, NW, Washington, DC 20049, "A Product Report on the Prepaying of Funerals."

Useful precautions include:

1. Accept only a plan that places a hundred percent of prepaid funds in trust, and only if there is adequate protection for such trust funds. An attorney's advice will be worthwhile to determine this.

2. Full refundability, transferability and the right of cancellation should be included. The funeral home one selects today may not be the one that one wants to do business with a year from now if it has been purchased by a conglomerate. Also, this gives necessary protection if someone dies while traveling.

3. You should receive an annual report showing where your money is, and how much is there. This is critical in states where there is no guarantee fund to protect customers in case of default. Only a few states have such protection: Florida, Indiana, Iowa, Missouri, North Carolina, Oregon, Texas, Vermont, and West Virginia. Hawaii and Virginia require some sort of bonding, but the amount does not appear to be adequate.

4. FCA and the American Association of Retired Persons suggest consulting a lawyer before signing any pre-need contract.

About Cremation

Modern cremation is a process for returning a body to its elements through intense heat and evaporation. It is completed in one to three hours and results in several pounds of bone fragments, usually called ashes or cremated remains. Crematories usually pulverize these fragments to reduce the volume, which is around two hundred cubic inches.

Cremation is an ancient practice dating back at least to biblical times when Saul and his sons were cremated, as recorded in the book of 1 Samuel, chapter 31. It has been practiced for thousands of years by Hindus and Buddhists, and was common in England from 787 A.D. Most religious groups, including the Roman Catholic Church, now permit cremation. The Greek Orthodox Church,

Conservative and Orthodox Jews as well as some conservative Protestant groups, Moslems, and Bahai's do not allow cremation.

Crematory charges average a little over two hundred dollars for just the cremation. (The charge at chain-owned crematories tends to be much higher.) Cost of a rigid, combustible, and covered container, transportation, paperwork, and miscellaneous services is additional. Many crematories and funeral directors can provide fiberboard body containers at a cost of from $25 to a $125. A plywood box can be built by the family. Most crematories charge extra for shipping the remains.

For several reasons, cremation is rapidly increasing in the United States, rising from about 5 percent of deaths in 1974 to nearly 24 percent in 1998, when there were 1,366 crematories in the United States, with an average of 407 cremations per crematory. The Cremation Association of North America predicts that cremation will be used in 40 percent of deaths by 2010.

Cremation normally costs less than earth burial if arrangements are made directly by the family or through a funeral director who works with a funeral consumer organization. The funeral director's charges for transportation and paperwork, however, are often more than the cost of cremation itself. A full-fledged funeral in the presence of the body may bring the cost of cremation into the same range as the cost of earth burial, though cost may be reduced by use of rental caskets. A memorial service, held after the body has been removed, as I explain in Chapter 7, "Death Ceremonies," not only saves expense but focuses attention on the life of the person instead of on the dead body.

For-Profit Cremation Services

In recent years private companies in many areas have offered the service of immediate body removal and cremation without embalming, sometimes (but not always!) at low cost. Some states have a special license for such "direct disposers." Some cremation services call themselves "societies," apparently taking advantage of the good reputation of "memorial societies," although they are actually private businesses. (Local nonprofit funeral consumer organizations were traditionally called "memorial societies." Most have followed the lead of the national organization, Funeral Consumers Alliance, in changing their names to avoid any confusion with the private businesses calling themselves "societies.")

Disposition of Cremated Remains

Cremated remains are usually white to gray in color and can be stored indefinitely. The crematory will return them in a prepurchased urn or in a container of cardboard, tin, or plastic, in which they may be mailed by registered mail and some express services. Some families prefer to scatter cremated remains in a favorite garden or woods, from a mountain top, at sea, or in a "scattering garden" within a cemetery. First be sure they are pulverized, to avoid visible bone fragments. Several states, including California, place restrictions on disposition of cremated remains. In California, the remains may be scattered at sea, interred in a cemetery, or kept at home.

Many church burial grounds and commercial cemeteries provide special areas for the disposition of cremated remains. Some provide scattering gardens, urn gardens for earth burial, and some have exterior or interior columbaria (structures containing niches for urns). Memorial gardens are becoming increasingly popular—cemeteries in which markers may be at ground level, providing a more parklike setting, or they may have markers placed on stone hedges surrounding a scattering area or urn garden. If you are considering such a disposition, take time to compare options and prices, as costs vary greatly.

Earth Burial

Earth burial is still the most common form of body disposition in the United States and Canada. Burial may be in commercial cemeteries, church cemeteries, or (in some states) family burying grounds or individually owned land. Traditional cemeteries allow families to select any gravestone they like. Memorial parks require that stones be level with the ground.

Prices for grave plots vary from about $150 to $1,500 or more. Opening and closing grave costs are similar, with an extra charge for weekends or holidays. Concrete grave liners are required by most cemeteries to prevent the ground above the grave from sinking with time. Concrete or metal vaults may also be used as grave liners; some are guaranteed waterproof for a period of years and costs range up to $2,000 and more. Some of these are sold with the erroneous claim that they will preserve the body. Some people choosing earth burial prefer that their bodies return to the earth in a natural manner, and therefore use wood or corrugated boxes. Simple grave markers cost a minimum of $250 plus engraving.

Transporting of Bodies

Sometimes a body needs to be transported for a ceremony or interment in a distant place. If a common carrier is to be used, a funeral director will know what to do. Before using an air express service, check with Amtrak. It offers quick service to many destinations and is much cheaper than air. Unless waived for religious reasons, embalming is often required for transport by common carrier.

Handling of transportation by members of the family can be both emotionally wholesome and economical. If the body is to be transported by the family in a suitable vehicle, a death certificate and transportation permit must be obtained according to local regulations. County registrars, health departments, coroners, and funeral directors can provide information on regulations. Lisa Carlson's *Caring for the Dead* provides detailed state-by-state information on regulations and procedures; see Bibliography at end of chapter. All states honor the proper permits from other states when a body is moved. Depending on the weather and the distance to be traveled, embalming or dry ice may be needed. There may be local regulations that necessitate such measures as embalming or hermetic sealing of the casket. This can be talked over with the health department.

Nonprofessional Funerals

Some groups and individuals care for their own dead without the assistance of a funeral director. A few are religious groups such as the Quakers or Mennonites. Others are rural families, particularly in Appalachia. Some are organized within the framework of a funeral consumer organization, like the one that served as an adviser to the Natural Deathcare Project in northern California. Each operates within the laws of its own state, which vary widely.

While individuals can successfully care for their dead in many areas, it is highly desirable for families who wish to do this to join forces with other members of their church or local community. Moral support is an important factor. The first time the burial committee of the Yellow Springs (Ohio) Friends Meeting had occasion to care for one of their dead, we received a sharp response from the funeral directors who, together with a representative of the state board, descended upon us. Fortunately, our group contained several substantial citizens and had carefully researched the matter in advance. We explained to our visitors our philosophy and the laws of Ohio, whereupon they smiled and politely went away. This would have been more difficult for a single family. Since that time, using this as a precedent, some individual Ohio families have cared for their own dead without group assistance.

Requirements vary from state to state, and crematories and cemeteries may have rules of their own. These laws and regulations— generally public health statutes and regulations governing licensing and operations of funeral directors, cemeteries, and crematories—must be carefully checked. Information for all states is provided in Carlson's *Caring for the Dead*. She has found that the only states still *requiring* at least some involvement by a funeral director are Nebraska, New York, Louisiana, Connecticut and Indiana. Carlson attributes these limitations to funeral director lobbying, combined with lack of information to legislators, adding that the restrictions appear to conflict with Constitutional rights and therefore may be subject to court challenges.

For instructions on building inexpensive burial boxes, see Appendix 5, "Simple Burial."

An Example

The burial committee of the Yellow Springs Friends Meeting has functioned successfully for forty-five years. Member families fill out forms in advance, authorizing the committee to act on their behalf, and include the necessary biographical data and endorsement by the next of kin. The form is shown in Appendix 5, "Simple Burial."

When a death occurs, a member of the committee gets the death certificate signed by the attending physician or coroner and takes it to the health department to be recorded. The committee keeps blank death certificate forms on hand. The next of kin signs an authorization to cremate and makes out a check to the crematory, if cremation is desired. Burial or removal to a medical school follows much the same pattern. Committee members serve without pay, which minimizes the possibility of legal complications.

At the same time that the disposition of the body is being handled, committee members assist the family with food, baby-sitting, hospitality for relatives, getting out death notices, and helping to plan a suitable memorial service. This support is very meaningful.

This committee and its arrangements did not come into being overnight. The committee had examined the laws and explained their plans carefully to the state and local departments of health. They set up advance arrangements with a crematory and visited each of the nearby hospitals so that there would be no misunderstanding or delay when a death occurred.

An example of a simple, nonprofessional burial was the occasion of my first wife's death. The burial committee of the Celo (North Carolina) Friends Meeting quietly functioned. Friends and students at the Arthur Morgan School quickly built a box from materials already at hand and cut to size. They dug a grave in the Friends' burial ground, arranged a graveside committal service followed later by a memorial service, and assisted the family in various other ways. The whole thing was beautifully handled, conveying a warm feeling of fellowship and support. My total cash expense was twenty-three dollars for plywood plus a two-dollar filing fee.

The Coroner's Role

It is important to understand the role of the coroner if there is one in your county. His responsibility is to check on accidental deaths, homicides, suicides, and sudden or unexpected deaths—especially when no physician has been in attendance. It is mandatory that all such deaths be reported to him promptly. It is his job to determine the cause of death and whether there has been foul play. He should be given active cooperation. A friend of mine, a Christian Scientist, died without benefit of a physician. His family wished to handle arrangements without a funeral director but didn't realize they needed a death certificate from the coroner. This got them into some embarrassing difficulty that, fortunately, the Yellow Springs Friends Meeting burial committee was able to resolve.

Death in a Foreign Country

Some eight thousand Americans die in foreign countries each year. Everyone going abroad should carry in their passports instructions to be followed in the event of death. This should be done regardless of age or good health and should be discussed with families before leaving, to avoid conflicting instructions. A second choice should be indicated in case the first is not available. The full name of father, maiden name of mother, full (maiden) name of spouse, date and place of birth, and occupation should be listed. The exact location of any will should be included, along with the name of the executor, if any.

If someone dies abroad while accompanied by an adult member of the immediate family, that family member will make the arrangements. The nearest American consular office should be contacted and can give advice. If no adult family member is along, the consular office is responsible to notify the next of kin in the United States and then carry out their instructions concerning disposition of the body. The consul will furnish a "report of death," which has the legal status of a death certificate. The consul is also prepared to serve as provisional conservator (not administrator) of the deceased's property in the foreign country. A small percentage fee is charged for this.

Advance payment in full is normally required for disposition of the body. If instructions or payment is not received in a reasonable length of time, the consular office allows local authorities to dispose of the body as unclaimed.

Cremation in countries with facilities for it is usually cheaper than burial. If cremation is not available in the country where death occurred, it may be available in a nearby country. Costs vary greatly. In the Sudan, a cremation costs $60; in France, $1,500. Ashes may, if desired, be sent home by mail. Earth burial is universally available and varies greatly in cost. In some countries it may be cheaper than cremation.

If body donation for scientific or educational purposes is acceptable to the family this option should be pursued. In most foreign countries there is a serious shortage of cadavers. In some countries, as many as two hundred medical students have to share a single body for study.

Often, bodies of people who die abroad are flown home. This requires embalming, which is not always readily available, plus special packing and a hermetically sealed coffin plus an outside shipping case. This adds up to several thousand dollars. Consulates usually know which mortuaries are able to handle such complex shipments. It will normally be less costly to dispose of the body without shipping it home. If you prefer the cheapest way, be sure to say so. Don't hesitate to shop around.

What to Do When Death Occurs, if a Funeral Director is Used

A doctor or coroner must declare the person dead and sign a death certificate, which can be obtained from the hospital, health department, or funeral director.

When family members are ready to have the body taken away, the funeral director of their choice is called. See Chapter 2, "Living with Dying." The hospital or nursing home will do this for you if the death has occurred there. Funeral consumer organization members will call a funeral director who has a contract with or is recommended by their society. A clergyman, appropriate church or synagogue committee, or friend should be contacted promptly to help where necessary, and especially in making arrangements with the funeral director if there has been no advance planning. See pages 56–57.

Checklist of Things to Be Done

(You may wish to photocopy these pages and attach them to your plans for final arrangements.)

☐ Arrange for members of family or friends to take turns answering door or phone, keeping careful record of calls.

☐ Coordinate the supplying of food for the next days.

☐ Arrange appropriate child care.

☐ Decide on time and place of funeral or memorial service(s). See Chapter 7, "Death Ceremonies," pages 77–88.

☐ If flowers are to be omitted, decide on appropriate memorial to which gifts may be made (such as a church, library, school, or charity).

☐ Make list of immediate family, close friends, and employer or business colleagues. Notify each by phone.

☐ Prepare list of distant persons to be notified by letter or printed notice, and decide which to send each.

☐ Write obituary. Check cost with newspaper. Some newspapers charge as much as two hundred dollars or more for death notices. In this case, a written notice may be mailed to friends. If you submit a death notice to the paper, include age, place of birth, cause of death, occupation, college degree(s), memberships held, military service, outstanding work, and list of survivors in immediate family. Give time and place of services. Deliver in person or by phone to newspapers.

☐ Arrange for hospitality for visiting relatives and friends.

☐ Consider special needs of the household—for example, cleaning—that might be done by friends.

☐ Select pallbearers and notify them. See Chapter 7, "Death Ceremonies," page 77.

☐ If deceased was living alone, notify utilities and landlord, and tell post office where to send mail. Take precaution against thieves, especially during the time of the funeral or memorial service.

☐ Plan for disposition of flowers after funeral (for example, they might be sent to a hospital or rest home).

☐ Prepare list of persons to receive acknowledgments of flowers, calls, food, and anything else that needs thanks. Send appropriate notes. (Can be written notes, printed acknowledgments, or some of each.)

☐ Notify lawyer and executor. Get several copies of death certificate.

☐ Check carefully all insurance (life and casualty) and death benefits, including Social Security, credit union, trade union, fraternal, military, or any other special interest group that might pay benefits to survivors of the deceased. Check also on income for survivors from these sources. See pages 57–58.

☐ Check promptly on all debts and installment payments. Some may carry insurance clauses that will cancel them. If there is to be a delay in meeting payments, consult with creditors and ask for more time before the payments are due.

Planning for Inheritance—Keeping Down Legal Costs

Survivorship can be enormously simplified if the person who has died has taken the trouble to discuss these financial matters with his or her family and make appropriate plans. Failure to do so can lead to conflict and much unnecessary work and expense.

Everyone who owns property should make a will, carefully determining what he or she wants to do and paying a competent attorney to draw up the document. If a person dies without a will, his or her property will be distributed in accordance with state law, often not at all what the person would have chosen. An executor to administer the estate also should be selected in advance. If not provided in the will, an executor will be appointed by the court. Since each state has its own rules concerning wills, a will needs to be reviewed, and perhaps redrawn, if a person moves to a new state.

Careful estate planning may also minimize state and federal inheritance taxes and probate costs. There are many legal instruments for doing this, and tax laws frequently change. It is therefore advisable to consult an attorney to make one's plans.

Probate

Probate is a court proceeding to verify a will and clear title to property being inherited through a will or under the law of intestacy. Probate proceedings provide an orderly inheritance process, but may be very costly and time consuming (often at least a year).

Former U.S. Chief Justice Warren Burger once commented that standard legal fees charged to probate an estate after a death are frequently out of proportion to the value of the services rendered. These fees are in some cases well earned; in others they constitute a sheer windfall. Justice Burger remarked that the legal profession had allowed the "relatively simple business" of settling a will to "become encrusted with excess procedure baggage that . . . often adds unreasonably to costs." Often, a percentage of the value of the estate is charged, regardless of the amount of work involved. A helpful book is Norman F. Dacey's *How to Avoid Probate—Updated.*

While it is wise to use an attorney in these matters, a family may minimize legal fees by handling many of the details that usually take up much of the attorney's time, using the attorney in an advisory capacity and to handle the more technical matters. All records concerning finances, property, and insurance, should be kept in good order and readily accessible, as attorneys often spend much expensive time straightening out records. See "Write It Down!" page 56. It is entirely proper to negotiate with an attorney to pay only for the actual time spent. At present, fifty to seventy-five dollars an hour is not unreasonable. Better yet, arrange a flat fee for the job. Sometimes an experienced accountant can handle the entire process. For such work, especially if the accountant is a CPA, she or he should receive a comparable rate of pay.

Choosing a lawyer at a time of grieving can be stressful. To avoid this, it may be helpful to periodically discuss with a spouse which local lawyers seem to be good ones.

Beware of Vultures

Survivors, particularly widows, are commonly preyed upon by swindlers of one kind or another. A favorite device is to collect a nonexistent debt owed by the deceased, or to deliver merchandise (commonly a Bible) that was never ordered.

Another ploy is to inform the survivor of a nonexistent life insurance policy on which a final premium must be paid before benefits can be collected, or of some other valuable asset requiring a final payment of some kind. Widows are prime prospects for bad investments, and even reputable investment firms, when asked, will sometimes recommend changing stock portfolios merely for the sake of the commissions involved.

The moral is: be careful, go slow, and consult an experienced member of the family or other trusted business adviser.

BIBLIOGRAPHY/CHAPTER 5
(See also Appendices 5 and 6, especially FCA publications.)

The American Funeral, LeRoy Bowman. Westport, CT: Greenwood Press, reprinted 1973. Classic sociological study.

FCA Newsletter. A quarterly, with the consumer viewpoint on events and trends in the funeral industry and the memorial society movement.

Caring for the Dead, Lisa Carlson. Hinesburg, VT: Upper Access Publishers (P.O. Box 457, 05461), 1998. A comprehensive tome on funeral law for the layperson. In addition to the do-it-yourself information, it covers cemetery and crematory laws and regulations, the detailed problems of prepaid funerals, and much more.

The American Way of Death Revisited, Jessica Mitford. New York: Knopf, 1998. A classic with important new information.

Death to Dust: What Happens to Dead Bodies, Kenneth Iserson. Tucson, AZ: Galen Press, 1994. An extensive coverage of what happens to the body after death, including in-depth information about embalming, cremation, cryogenic preservation, autopsies, organ donation, anatomical dissection, burials, and funerals.

How to Avoid Probate—Updated, Norman Dacey. New York: Crown Publishers, Inc., revised, 1987. Has helped many families reduce legal costs following death. Explains the process of probate and provides forms for filing an "inter vivos" trust. Helpful only if used before death.

The Truth About Funerals, Dan Flynn, Funeral Consultants International, P.O. Box 85119, Burlington, ON, Canada L7R 4KB. A funeral director comes to the aid of the consumer.

A supplementary source of information is the FCA Web site, which offers a gold mine of information at no cost: htttp://www.funerals.org.

6 FUNERAL CONSUMER ORGANIZATIONS

As author of A Manual of Simple Burial, *I was invited in 1963 to attend the founding meeting of the Continental Association of Funeral and Memorial Societies and served for many years on its board of directors.* The Manual, *now in its fourteenth edition and renamed* Dealing Creatively with Death, *has served as source book and advocate for the memorial society movement since its inception..*

Memorial Societies, or More Accurately, Funeral Consumer Organizations

For more than fifty years these organizations, calling themselves memorial societies, have been performing an important service in the United States and Canada. But now Lisa Carlson, the executive secretary of the Funeral Consumer Alliance (FCA), points out that some organizations of funeral directors have usurped the name "memorial society."

That puts our movement in a difficult position. The most obvious solution, suggested by Lisa, is to start shifting the names of our organizations to the title listed above. This doesn't have to be done suddenly, but we should be getting about it, and all new organizations should take note of it. The directory of existing organizations can be found in Appendix 6.

What They Are and How They Work

Memorial societies / funeral consumer organizations are cooperative nonprofit consumer groups, democratically run, that help their members to get dignity and economy in funeral arrangements through advance planning. They are not run by funeral directors.

These groups themselves generally do not offer funeral services but act in an advisory capacity and often have contracts or agreements with funeral directors on behalf of their members. Thus they help their members to get exactly the services they want, and at reasonable cost. The work of the groups is done by unpaid volunteers in most cases; a few of the larger organizations have paid secretaries.

These organizations do collectively what few individual families are prepared to do—they inquire around, compare services and prices, then share this information with their members. They do *not* collect payment for funeral services. For information on alternatives for the disposition of bodies, see Chapter 5, "Simple Burial and Cremation."

There are local or regional groups in about 150 cities in North America, with a combined membership of over half a million. Most societies charge a one-time membership fee of from fifteen to thirty dollars, and some have a small records charge, which they collect from the family at time of death, via the funeral director. A few have a small *annual* membership fee or solicit voluntary annual contributions. All societies effect large savings for their members and are an outstanding example of how consumers, by democratic group effort, can empower themselves at the grassroots level.

Memorial Services

In addition to advising their members on funeral arrangements, these societies can often help with suggestions for memorial services. See also Chapter 7, "Death Ceremonies."

Membership Is Transferable

Families moving to another city can transfer their membership at little or no charge. Likewise, when a death occurs away from home, the society in the host city and its cooperating funeral director will assist the family.

History

The practice of group planning for funeral arrangements started early in the century in the farm Grange organization in the northwestern United States. From there the idea spread to the cities, mainly under church leadership. The People's Memorial Association of Seattle, organized in 1939, was the first urban group. Organizations spread gradually up and down the West Coast, then eastward across the United States, and again northward into Canada.

Funeral Consumers Alliance (FCA)

By 1963 the societies had become a strong continent-wide movement, and the Cooperative League of the U.S.A. called a meeting in Chicago, where Canadian and U.S. societies together formed the Continental Association of Funeral and Memorial Societies (CAFMS). The Canadian societies later separated, as their concerns did not always coincide with those of the U.S. groups, and CAFMS changed its name to FAMSA (Funeral and Memorial Societies of America.)

In 1999, after research showed that most Americans confused FAMSA with industry organizations, the name was changed again, this time to Funeral Consumers Alliance (FCA).

The member societies, and literature available from FCA, are listed in Appendix 6, "Directory of Funeral Consumer Organizations." FCA serves as a central clearinghouse for information and publicity and assists new organizations in forming. In several states where there are a number of societies, state federations have been organized to follow consumer issues within the state and to act as needed.

Having a strong central office, FCA is the principal advocate for the consumer of funeral services. In this capacity it speaks not only for its immediate membership, but for the 247 million Americans who are not members, all of whom must someday die. (Each year 3.3 million Americans die.) Working closely with the Federal Trade Commission FCA (then called CAFMS) was instrumental in securing passage—after a long struggle—of the Funeral Rule requiring funeral directors to quote prices freely and to offer their services on an itemized basis, rather than as package deals. This does not tell people what kind of funerals they should have, but broadens their opportunity for choice and opens up important savings options.

Friends of FCA

This is a national organization of individuals and families who do not have access to a local society. They have all rights of membership in the local organizations, and membership can be transferred to any of the local FCA affiliates. (See Page 54.)

How to Organize a Funeral Consumer Organization

An organizational guidebook for running such a society is available for ten dollars from FCA. In addition, FCA has persons experienced in society organization, who are often able to give a hand in helping new societies to get started.

Financial Savings

Memorial society members commonly save fifty to seventy-five percent of usual funeral costs, with total savings to members of millions of dollars annually. In 1997 the People's Memorial Association of Seattle (PMA), the largest society in the United States, had a contract for funeral service and burial ranging from $650 to $950, to be compared with an average cost for an adult funeral of $5,500 to $6,500, when costs include cemetery costs. For the eighty-five percent of PMA members electing cremation, the contracted price is $530. An average of about six thousand services are provided to PMA members annually, helping to make funeral costs on the West Coast the lowest in the United States. These savings resulted in part from collective bargaining, but more from the simplicity that members are encouraged to practice.

Cooperation With Funeral Directors

In many cases, societies negotiate contracts or agreements with funeral directors, through which the society members can get (only) the services they desire, and at predetermined prices. While funeral directors originally took a dim view of memorial societies, arrangements between funeral directors and the local groups generally have proved satisfactory to all concerned.

In cases where no contracts or agreements can be arranged, societies are generally able to advise their members where to turn to get the services and prices they want. In a couple of cases where funeral directors refused to cooperate at all, the societies found ways to bypass them altogether.

The Social Base of Funeral Consumer Organizations

By and large it has been prosperous, educated, middle-class families who have organized these societies—doctors, lawyers, teachers, business people. Mostly they have been church people, too, and mainly concerned with simplicity. Ironically, working-class families and minority ethnic groups, on whom the burden of funeral costs falls most heavily, have been less inclined to join these groups.

Society leaders have been concerned with this and have kept the doors of membership open to all. Some societies actively seek members and leadership from minority groups and the less affluent, with modest success in recent years.

Imitation Societies

The success and popularity of memorial societies have led to imitations. Private companies calling themselves "societies" have entered the funeral service business in various places. Some offer what they term "direct cremation" services. This is a valid form of disposition of human remains, but it is misleading for such firms to call themselves societies. As noted previously, this deception has led the national organization, and many local memorial societies, to change their names. Nevertheless, the local consumer organizations are still widely known as "societies," so private companies continue their attempts to confuse the public.

If someone from a privately owned "society" tries to sell you something or offers you a prepayment plan, investigate carefully. Memorial societies (or local funeral consumer organizations) have no commercial interests and rarely charge membership fees over thirty dollars. In general, true memorial societies advise against prepayment plans. There are various ways to make advance financial provision for death. See Chapter 5, "Simple Burial and Cremation," pages 57–60.

All bona fide societies in the United States are members of FCA. When in doubt about a society, check in the directory in Appendix 6, "Directory of Funeral Consumer Organizations," to see if it is a member, or contact FCA.

7   DEATH CEREMONIES

I heartily agree with funeral directors that ceremonies at a time of death are important in meeting the social and emotional needs of survivors. This chapter presents the viewpoint, however, that effective and appropriate ceremonies are possible with very little expense. And that conversely, elaborate and expensive ceremonies may distract attention from the meaning and value of the life of the one who has died.

The chapter includes detailed instruction on many aspects of death ceremonies, particularly encouraging participation of family and friends in whatever type of service is chosen. Appendix 7, "Sample Death Ceremonies," includes sample ceremonies and readings that may be used.

Much of the work of preparing this chapter was done by Ann Baty, of the Bowling Green Memorial Society, who studied the subject over a period of years and corresponded with hundreds of clergy and lay people. Valuable ideas were derived also from Dr. LeRoy Bowman's The American Funeral, which remains an authoritative source after forty-six years, and from my own experience.

Humankind, from earliest times, has practiced death ceremonies and procedures in great variety. The reason for these ceremonies is not hard to understand. Such procedures are important to the healing process. No human being lives in a social vacuum; our speech, habits, values—the very meaning of life—derive from our association with one another. Hence the death of one individual is traumatic for the survivors. Recognizing that death ceremonies and related customs are important in meeting the social and emotional needs of survivors, we should plan these ceremonies carefully.

In recent years there has been a worldwide move towards deritualized funerals (and other ceremonies, too). Our purpose in this section of *Dealing Creatively* is not to weaken or eliminate ritual but to help create more meaningful rituals.

Needs to Be Met by Death Ceremonies

Every situation is different, with different circumstances, different personalities, and different needs. Here are some of the needs that are commonly found, and ways in which appropriate ceremonies can help meet them.

Reestablishing Relationships. Death, like marriage, changes a broad range of relationships, as between parent and child, brother and sister, and friends. After a death in the family we are not quite the same people we were before. We therefore must rediscover ourselves in a new set of relationships. This relates directly to the process of mourning.

A promising child of a prominent family had died suddenly, to the great shock of the family and community. A simple service had been held with just the family and a few close friends. Then, for days afterward, as the mother encountered other good friends, each felt the necessity of conveying sympathy, at the expense of unhappiness to themselves and of rubbing fresh salt in the wounds of the mother.

Had the service been open to all, in quarters large enough to receive the friends, the individual condolences could have been replaced by a single meeting, the relationships reestablished, and life resumed in a more normal way.

Identification. The ceremony can cultivate a sense of identity with the deceased. The survivors can be helped to recognize that they have shared the person's life and that they are now, in their own lives, the custodians of the values that he or she lived by. In a sense, their lives can be a memorial.

A young man whose career had been joyously and usefully devoted to human service had died. Entering the church for the funeral service, his stricken parents appeared utterly crushed and forlorn.

In the audience were a large number of young people who had known this man and shared his concerns. The speaker talked of the young man's life and what he stood for and went on to say that his ideals and spirit were alive and growing in each of those present. In a very real sense, said the speaker, his effective work was just beginning, and would go forward in the lives of his friends. The response of the listeners could be seen in their faces; most of all, in the faces of the parents. Leaving the church, they were almost radiant and one of them remarked, "Wasn't it fine?" Suddenly all these young people had become, in spirit, their children.

Affirmation of Values. It is almost a universal experience that at time of death survivors are prone to think seriously of the meaning of life and to meditate on its values. They are at that time not only open to inspiration but hungry for it. The occasion, therefore, should be used for the enrichment and refinement of life. This is perhaps the most enduring comfort that can be given.

Relief of Guilt. At a time of death, the surviving members of the family are commonly torn between their feelings of love and grief, and the shock and revulsion they tend to feel in the presence of the dead body. It is normal, in this situation, for them to recall their shortcomings with respect to the deceased and to reproach themselves. No human relationship is perfect. A wife recalls how she scolded poor Henry for tracking in mud. Children remember how they neglected their parents. A husband remembers that Mary never did get that trip to the seashore that she wanted so much. "But it's too late now."

Apparently, this is usual. Certainly it is the major basis of many costly and ostentatious funerals. One of the functions of death ceremonies is to gently and quietly remove this sense of guilt through the process of reaffirmation of the values of the deceased. Perhaps the strongest force in lifting the sense of guilt is the reacceptance that the survivors experience from their friends. Love and solidarity help greatly. A thoughtfully planned service provides an excellent opportunity to express this.

Rehabilitation. When an old person dies after his or her powers have declined greatly from their prime, it is helpful to the survivors to have the memory of this person redirected to the better years of his or her life. Before my father-in-law died, his mental powers had failed and life had become an unhappy burden. His death produced a mixture of grief and thankfulness accompanied by a certain amount of guilt. There was no viewing of the remains. At the memorial service, we brought into focus what he was and what he had done in earlier years. From that day we carried with us the image of the fine strong person he had been. No amount of cosmetic restoration could have taken the place of that. In fact, any viewing would have detracted from the desired effect.

Religious Observance. The occasion of death is an important time to deepen spiritual life, draw on the strength of religious experience and tradition, and unify a congregation. Services planned with the family's clergyman and held in a house of worship can help greatly in this process.

Emotional Support. A death in the family is like an amputation. The survivors have lost part of themselves and experience intense loneliness and insecurity. The gathering of family, friends, and community can be a great source of encouragement and strength. This rallying of support, I might add, should not wait for the funeral or memorial service. Family members and close friends should visit promptly.

A State Funeral. On the death of a prominent person with whom many people had a meaningful emotional relationship, there is need for a ceremony in which large numbers of people can take part.

An outstanding case in which these needs were sensitively met was the funeral of President John F. Kennedy. The casket was not opened for public viewing. There were no truckloads of flowers in the funeral procession. Since the entire nation felt a close connection with President Kennedy, an impressive ceremony, widely televised, in which the whole nation could participate, was in good taste and filled an important need.

Three Types of Death Ceremonies

A *funeral service* is, by definition, a service held in the presence of the body, with either an open or closed casket. A *memorial service* is, by definition, a service held after the body has been removed. It can be either a substitute for a funeral service or in addition to it. A *commitment*, or *committal service* is a brief, optional service held at the graveside or in the chapel of a crematory. It is usually in addition to a funeral or memorial service and is the occasion at which the immediate family and possibly a few close friends bid good-bye to the body.

Ministers and funeral directors are trained in conducting funeral and committal services, but not all have had experience with memorial services. Most of this chapter, therefore, is devoted to memorial services.

Funeral and Committal Services

First, however, I want to offer a few comments on funeral and committal services. These have greater possibilities for variety and for survivor participation than are usually realized. They may be programmed closely or may provide for spontaneous participation.

Many years ago, a young priest in Hays, Kansas, read the *Manual* and liked the idea of participation by funeral attenders. He designed a model funeral service that was performed at a national meeting of the Catholic Art Association, in which I took part. The service proved to be a skillful blending of Catholic ritual with Quaker sharing of testimony. I recall also an excellent Quaker funeral, with a closed casket, at which the funeral director presided and the attenders, including the husband of the woman who had died, did the speaking as they felt moved.

At a funeral, the choice of pallbearers should favor members of the family who may wish to take part. Instead of civic leaders and business associates, the family should have the first chance—including women and teenagers. I have known women who felt deeply deprived because they were excluded from this privilege. The less husky pallbearers should be distributed so that they don't have to lift too much. Indeed, if the box is too heavy, it suggests that the family may have been extravagant in choosing it. Remember also to be careful not to call upon persons with serious heart or back problems. There are more such than we commonly realize.

At a committal service, too, there can be family participation. At my first wife's interment I recited one of her favorite poems and helped lower the box into the ground. Family members may be encouraged to start filling in the grave. Such things are emotionally helpful to the survivors.

An important decision to be made in planning a funeral service is the choice between an open or closed casket. It is the overwhelming preference of clergymen—Protestant, Catholic, and Jewish—that the casket be closed. In many cases the viewing of the remains is confined to family members and takes place before the funeral. When family members have been with the body at death or soon after, no later viewing is necessary.

A good "memory image," as funeral directors call it, may be created without viewing the body. Personal reminiscences of the living person can usually generate a better image than viewing the "restored" body.

There are, however, times when cosmetic restoration can be helpful, as when relatives from far away wish to see the body. This does not necessarily require a public viewing. Sensitivity to the wishes of the family should be the key to decisions in this matter.

If a service is held with the casket present, it may be covered with a gray cloth (or pall) as is done, for instance, in Episcopal churches. Thus a solid bronze casket carries no more prestige than a plywood box. This symbolizes the belief that we are all equal in death and helps focus on the spiritual significance of the occasion.

Memorial Services

A memorial service performs much the same function as a funeral service, but tends to have a more positive atmosphere. This is mainly because it is focused on the values of the person who has died instead of on the dead body.

Members of the family should be encouraged—but never pressured —to speak or to offer songs or prayers as they may choose. The following experience is an example of how helpful a memorial service can be, with appropriate family participation.

A friend of mine lost a grown daughter in an automobile accident. He loved her dearly, but there had been some stress between them, and this made her death doubly hard for him. I went to see him and his wife. It happened that I, too, had lost a daughter sometime before in a similar accident.

The family were not members of the Society of Friends, but I offered to arrange a memorial service in the Friends meetinghouse and suggested that the father might like to speak at such a meeting. They accepted the offer, but he wasn't sure he would be able to speak. He called me shortly afterward, however, and said he did indeed want to speak and wanted me to preside.

At the service, the meeting room was decorated with wild flowers and on the mantel was a painting done by the young woman. Her former music teacher played a piece she had especially liked. Then I spoke, saying that we had gathered in the girl's memory and that any who felt moved to speak should feel free to do so. Then the father got up. In his hand was a bunch of little cards, each with a reminder of some incident from his daughter's life, starting from early childhood. He spoke with difficulty at first, but soon became more fluent. As he continued to relate happy memories, a faraway look came into his eyes and he began to smile, and the assembled friends smiled with him.

His wife thought he was speaking too long and tried to catch his eye, but their son, seated next to her, said, "Let him talk." And he did, for quite a while. When he sat down there was a period of silence, then their friends spoke in turn, spontaneously, words of comfort and philosophy and reminiscence. When the speaking ran its course and the service was over, it was dark outside. We carried a few chairs into the yard and set candles on them. Friends moved freely inside and outside, visiting with the family and each other. That meeting was, as any good funeral or memorial service should be, the point at which the family could begin to resume normal life and look to the future. They expressed the warmest appreciation.

There was an interesting sequel when, a few weeks later, the father had occasion to attend the funeral of a business colleague. It was a strictly conventional service at which the minister delivered a cut-and-dried oration—and that was it. My friend was struck by the contrast between the services and was angry at the impersonal and empty character of his friend's funeral.

Self-Planned Services

Some people like to plan their own services. These may be regular funeral services for which the person has selected the readings and music and even, perhaps, the persons to do the readings. Some have planned that their family and friends shall simply come together for a social evening in their memory, with refreshments and fellowship, and perhaps entertainment arranged by the one who has died. Some people make recordings of readings or music to be played at their funeral or memorial services.

Multiple Services

It is often desirable to hold more than one gathering in cases where different groups or distant places are involved. On the occasion of my first wife's death, one gathering was held in North Carolina and another in Ohio, and I spoke at both.

Sometimes friends or colleagues in a remote place hold a memorial service independently. This should be fully reported to the family, who will take comfort from it.

No Service at All

Is it ever appropriate to have no funeral or memorial service at all? Yes, under some circumstances this is entirely appropriate. For instance, if the person wanted it that way, the family may properly comply with that wish.

Recently, a young man was killed in an accident two thousand miles from his parents' home. It had been years since he had lived with his parents. His work kept him moving from place to place and he had lost contact with his boyhood friends. His parents quite properly decided not to hold a formal service. Friends of the family called at their home to express their love and sympathy.

While death ceremonies do in most cases meet an important need, the decision not to hold a service in a particular situation may be entirely appropriate.

Combination Programs

A mixture of programming and spontaneous contributions is often a good arrangement. Commonly, the program starts with music while people are gathering. If family members or friends are musicians, it is appropriate for them to play. Personal participation is more important than the technical excellence of recorded music. The latter can be used if no musicians are available.

After the opening music an appropriate reading is in order, either poetry or prose. Best of all is some bit of inspirational writing by the person who has died, if this is available. A few suitable selections are offered in Appendix 7, "Sample Death Ceremonies."

Following the reading, a brief talk may be given relating to the person who has died. This can be followed by more music and another reading. Attenders can then be invited to share their thoughts, feelings, and memories. When this seems to have run its course, there can be more music followed, if desired, by a prayer and/or a period of silence. Attenders should be invited to remain afterward to visit.

Ceremonies on the Death of the Very Young

The tragic death of a young child presents special problems because of the greater guilt and anger often mingled with the family's grief. If the memorial service is handled wisely, the love the parents had for the child often can be channeled into greater affection for one another and for their surviving children. A minister conducting a service can develop this concept, or an attender can, if the service allows for participation.

The death ceremony for a baby will naturally be less extensive than for an adult or older child, though it should provide an opportunity for friends to give emotional support. It is important to have a ceremony, if only a modest one.

In the case of a stillborn infant, it is well for the family to have a simple ceremony of their own, giving the child a name, recognizing it as a member of the family, and honoring its birth and death. Miscarriages and abortions also involve grief, and an informal ceremony can be very helpful. See Chapter 3, "Bereavement," for additional suggestions.

How to Plan a Service

Ideally the family should sit down together, along with their clergyman if they have one, and talk it over. Ann Baty describes this well: "You reminisce, you recall things he said, things he wrote, his ideals, his goals, his plans, his affections—even the annoying things he did. You look over old snapshots. You talk about him and you think about him. From these reflections you begin to plan your ceremony of remembrance." This is a wholesome process that can do much to begin emotional healing.

Time. The time usually preferred for a memorial service is the same as for a funeral service—two or three days after the death. Evenings and weekends are preferable so that more people can attend. The timing may be modified to meet individual situations, as, for instance, if some member of the family is in the hospital or too far away to come until later. Additional ceremonies at a later date may be appropriate. After my father's death there were two memorial gatherings, followed seven months later by a two-day convocation in his memory attended by family and colleagues from far and wide.

Place. The place of meeting, too, depends on circumstances and should accommodate the expected attendance. To assemble a handful of people in a large hall or sanctuary is forlorn. To turn people away for lack of space is even worse. A familiar place is good. It may be a church or a living room—or even outdoors.

The Format of a Memorial Service

Here are a few basic components with which a memorial service may be planned and procedures to be considered. A service may be designed to use these components in any way the family prefers. Most religious groups have specific worship ceremonies for death, and a clergyman of that faith can assist in preparing and carrying out the plans.

Forms and liturgies may be adapted to include many of the following elements and will in turn suggest other forms and content. Most forms of ritual permit greater flexibility than is generally used. Don't be afraid to express your wishes and explore possibilities.

Instrumental Music. While people are gathering, it is often good to have some muted organ music, if in a church, or quiet recorded music elsewhere. Or the attenders can gather in silence and have the service begin with music. Music by family and friends is best of all.

I recall a memorial service in my own family, held in a yard beneath the trees, in which by prearrangement the sound of musical chimes from a nearby church (of a different denomination) came through the trees beautifully at just the right time. Music can be interspersed in the program, too, if desired, or used to close it.

Singing. This is a very desirable form of music for a service, since it allows for participation by family and friends. Unless the song or songs are well known to the attenders, it is good to have song sheets or hymn books available. If printed or duplicated programs are used, words of the songs may be included. Solo or ensemble singing can have a place, especially if done by friends or members of the family. Always encourage family participation.

The Presiding Function. One individual, generally a minister or a friend of the family, customarily presides, stating the purpose of the gathering and setting the program in motion. This person may or may not also contribute remarks, readings and prayers. If attenders are invited to take part, the presiding person will explain when and how this is to be done. The presiding person also signals the end of the service.

Prayers. For many families, depending on their practice and belief, this is an important part of the service. Prayers may be offered by the minister or other presiding person or by any family member or friend.

Biographical Remarks. It is often appropriate to give a biographical account of the person's life at the outset of the service. This adds interest and meaning to the service and provides an opportunity for family participation.

Reminiscences. Whether programmed or unprogrammed, these add greatly to the service and help to convey in depth some feeling of the person's life and values. Family members especially should be encouraged to offer their thoughts and rememberings.

Sometimes, certain family members and friends are asked specifically to contribute their recollections, and these are scheduled in sequence to be the main part of the program. I recall a fine memorial service in which a series of speakers had the same topic: "I remember Charlotte."

Don't avoid humorous reminiscences or incidents that may have involved some frustration. If presented in good taste, these carry overtones of affection and a fuller picture of the person's life and personality.

Visual Materials. The use of films, slides, or pictures is sometimes appropriate, if such material is available. A family member, preferably, should do the narrating. A small display of photographs from the life of the person is always appropriate. Sometimes the family likes to have articles present that remind them of the person who has died and that add a touch of intimacy or color. This may take the form of craft or artwork, a favorite toy in the case of a child, or something connected with an adult's hobby or profession.

Silence. Though most commonly associated with Quakers, this practice is observed in many groups, with a period of silence included as part of the service.

Readings. There is a wealth of beautiful and inspiring poetry, prose, and scripture to draw upon. The Bible is a rich source. Likewise the writings of Kahlil Gibran, Rabindranath Tagore, and others. These readings can be programmed or, in the case of unprogrammed services, they can be offered by attenders. It is very appropriate to include writings of the person who has died, if available. A few selected readings and sources are listed in Appendix 7, "Sample Death Ceremonies."

Unprogrammed Contributions. These may constitute the entire service, following the opening music, perhaps a biographical sketch, and introductory remarks in which the attenders are invited to speak. Or they may be called for later in the service or omitted entirely. It is good for the presiding person to suggest that at least a short period of silence be allowed between speakings.

Care should be taken that time for unprogrammed contributions not be cut short. I have known family members who carried regrets for years that they were cut off from speaking because the service was "running too long."

A word of caution: If the attenders are unfamiliar with the practice of unprogrammed speaking, it may be good to have a few people prepared in advance to begin the speaking.

Visiting After the Service. It is often desirable for attenders to have an opportunity to visit informally after the service, if facilities allow for this.

Refreshments. The serving of refreshments during the visiting is a pleasant practice that facilitates conversation. Some may wish to serve a meal after the funeral or memorial service. The custom of the funeral feast is well known. In theory this is supplied by the family of the deceased, but in common practice, it is thoughtful friends and neighbors who supply the food and do the work.

Flexibility

Established procedures are often useful, but they need not be binding. One memorial service was held with everyone seated in a circle. At the close of the service they all stood and joined hands to sing a final song together. Another service (for a golfer) was held as a walking party across a golf course, winding up at the clubhouse for refreshments. Another took the form of a reception at the home of the family whose member had died.

Printed Programs

Programs are not necessary, but sometimes are nice to have. If a service is largely unprogrammed, there is no need for a printed program. If it is highly programmed, and especially if it involves group singing, then a program including the words of songs can be helpful. This will depend partly on the availability of duplicating equipment. If the service is held in a church, the church may have printed program blanks that can be used. A longer program, perhaps with the full text of the ceremony, also can be used as a death announcement to mail to those who could not attend. This may include a biographical sketch and some personal tributes.

Remember

Grief has many dimensions, which are experienced by different people in different ways. Likewise, death ceremonies take many forms. As Ann Baty says, do not be coerced into passive acceptance of a conventional pattern; do not be afraid to be creative. Remember that death is a natural event and an occasion for the honest expression of your deepest values.

BIBLIOGRAPHY/CHAPTER 7
(See also Appendices 1 and 7.)

Bittersweet . . . Hello, Goodbye, Sister Jane Marie Lamb, OP. Belleville, IL: SHARE National Office, 1988. An extensive resource in planning farewell rituals when a baby dies.

Bridging the Bereavement Gap: A Manual for the Preparation and Programming of Hospice Bereavement Services, Donna O'Toole. Burnsville, NC 28714: Compassion Books, 1985.

Final Celebrations, K. Sublette and M. Flagg. Ventura, CA: Pathfinder Publishing, 1992. A guide to assist individuals and families plan and personalize funeral and memorial ceremonies as a celebration of life.

Reminiscing Together, H. Thorsheim & B. Roberts. An instructive book of exercises and activities to strengthen memories. Written especially for those growing older, this book is rich in ideas on how people of all ages can access the past. Techniques are taught on how the senses can be used to stimulate memory— through photographs and pictures, songs and sounds, smells, tastes, and touch. Ideas throughout on the use of stories to bridge generations and build continuity and community with others.

Rituals for Living and Dying, David Feinstein and Peg Elliot Mayo. San Francisco: Harper San Francisco, 1992. The authors explain the importance and role of ritual in life and death and offer well-crafted step-by-step structured activities and wise insights to help readers confronting the grief of illness or loss to fashion rituals and rites of passage that nurture relationships, ease transitions, and feed the spirit. An insightful book for individuals and families facing loss and for those working with them.

8 HOW THE DEAD CAN HELP THE LIVING

This chapter is essentially a tract—an urgent appeal for human solidarity, to persuade people to think in terms of life and to share with the living any organs or tissues that, at the time of death, they or their loved ones no longer need. To bury or burn organs or tissues needed by the living is a form of blasphemy against life. Let us not be guilty of it. As for myself, I'm leaving my entire body for medical education.

This chapter sets forth the options and the procedures for various types of donations. Directories of medical schools and eye banks, addresses of helpful organizations, and information on transplantation of specific organs will be found in Appendix 8, "Anatomical Gifts."

Poet Robert Test states the issue beautifully:

The day will come when my body will lie upon a white sheet tucked neatly under the four corners of a mattress, located in a hospital busily occupied with the living and the dying. At a certain moment a doctor will determine that my brain has ceased to function and that, for all intents and purposes, my life has stopped.

When that happens, do not attempt to instill artificial life into my body by the use of a machine and don't call this my deathbed. Let it be called the Bed of Life, and let my body be taken from it to help others lead fuller lives.

Give my sight to the man who has never seen a sunrise, a baby's face, or love in the eyes of a woman. Give my heart to the person whose own heart has caused nothing but endless days of pain. Give my blood to the teenager who was pulled from the wreckage of his car, so that he may live to see his grandchildren play. Give my kidneys to a person who depends upon a machine to exist from week to week. Take my bones, every muscle, every fiber and nerve in my body, and find a way to make a crippled child walk. Explore every corner of my brain. Take my cells, if necessary, and let them grow so that, someday, a speechless boy will shout at the crack of a bat or a deaf girl will hear the sound of rain against her window.

Burn what is left of me and scatter the ashes to the winds to help the flowers grow.

If you must bury something, let it be my faults, my weaknesses, and all my prejudice against my fellow man.

Give my sins to the devil. Give my soul to God.

If, by chance, you wish to remember me, do it with a kind deed or word to someone who needs you. If you do all I have asked, I will live forever.[1]

Urgent Need for Anatomical Gifts

In the seventies, a historic breakthrough occurred in the transplanting of tissues and organs, starting with the use of cyclosporine. This is a drug that suppresses the immune system without leaving the patient vulnerable to infections as formerly.

In the eighties came the Belzer/UW organ preservation solution, which helps preserve organs and lets them function better and sooner after transplanting.

These and further advances have resulted in a tremendous increase in transplanting organs and tissues. In 1999, there were 21,692 life-saving organ transplants in the U.S.—kidneys, livers, pancreases, intestines, hearts, and lungs. But the waiting list of patients in June of 2000 numbered 70,240. In short, less than a third of the people in the U.S. who need organs, and who qualify medically for transplants, are able to receive them. Tens of thousands of them die needlessly.

Meanwhile, tissue transplants number in the hundreds of thousands. The numbers are not collected as methodically as for organ transplants, but again, supply falls severely short of the need. Tissue transplants include skin grafts for critically burned patients, donated corneas to avert or correct blindness, as well as donated bone, cartilage, and tendons to reconstruct and rehabilitate.[2]

Who May Donate?

Almost everyone is a potential donor. While younger persons are preferred for major organs, persons over sixty may contribute tissues such as corneas, middle ear tissue, bones, and skin. For most organs, donations are not accepted from a person who has a contagious or malignant disease or one who died of an unknown cause or who is at high risk of AIDS. Tissues from persons with some disabilities, such as Alzheimer's disease and ear disorders, are especially needed for research. Postmortem donation of artificial implants, with permission to analyze related tissues, can also be very helpful for research.

The donation of organs or tissues does not alter the appearance of the dead person at a funeral, nor does it cause him or her the slightest discomfort or inconvenience. The disturbance to the body is generally less than that involved in the routine process of embalming, unless an autopsy is performed as well. There is no cost for organ donation, but the family is still responsible for disposition of the body.

Most religious groups encourage donation. Some Moslem sects, however, do not permit it.

Bequeathal of Entire Body to a Medical School

Thousands of bodies are needed each year for the training of future doctors and dentists. New medical schools are opening, and the supply of unclaimed bodies is diminishing. Only the rapid increase in the practice of bequeathing bodies has averted a nationwide crisis. Bodies may only be given. They may not be sold. Bodies may be donated at death, or after a funeral, with or without viewing, if the funeral director follows the medical school's directions for embalming.

Alternative plans should always be made, through a funeral consumer organization if possible, as a medical school's decision to accept a body for study is usually made at the time of death, not before. If a bequeathal form has been filed with a medical school in advance, the school may accept the body even though its supplies are ample at the time.

Bequeathal of a body to a medical school, with a memorial service instead of a funeral service, saves the cost of a funeral. However, I recall the case of a man who bequeathed his body to save burial expense, but whose body was autopsied—which made his body unacceptable. As a result, he was given a conventional funeral—which bankrupted his family.

Most schools assume responsibility for the final disposition of the body, and will, if requested, return the ashes to the family. This may take as long as two years, but generally can be speeded up if desired.

How to Donate Tissues or Organs

There are several ways to donate tissues and organs. For addresses of these organizations, see Appendix 8, "Anatomical Gifts."

1. Discuss your wishes with your family, or others who have an emotional stake in this question. Doctors won't remove organs without family

approval, even if a donor card has been filled out. Be sure to inform your doctor, close friends, the matron of a nursing home, your executor—anyone who might be involved with handling your body. When admitted to a hospital, insist on your wishes being recorded on your patient chart.

2. For donating the entire body, see Appendix 8, "Anatomical Gifts," for instructions on how to make arrangements, together with a directory of medical schools, their degree of need, and their provision for transportation, or call the Living Bank 800-528-2971 for information.

3. Carry a Uniform Donor Card signed by yourself and two witnesses. This is legal authority for donation under the Canadian Human Tissue Gift Acts and the U.S. Anatomical Gifts Acts. *Be sure a twenty-four-hour number to call is provided* and carry the card with your driver's license, where it will readily be found in case of accident. See Appendix 8, "Anatomical Gifts," for sources for donor cards.

4. Check the space provided on the driver's license in most states and provinces.

5. Register with the Living Bank (see End Notes for this chapter) and carry their donor card with their twenty-four-hour, toll-free number. They have over 330,000 members. If called at the time of death, they will immediately contact the nearest appropriate facility to arrange for such anatomical gifts as were desired by the donor. They work with regional and national networks and are especially strategic in rural areas and smaller cities. They receive no tax support. We suggest a contribution if you send for their material.

6. Persons with allergies or other special medical conditions are well advised to register this information with Medic Alert and wear the tag or bracelet they provide. In an emergency they can be called collect for the necessary information, including, if desired, your anatomical gift wishes.

7. For information in Canada, contact Organ Donors Canada, Transplant International, or the transplant coordinator in one of the regional transplant coordinating centers.

Permission for Autopsy

Another service the dead and their families can render is permission for autopsy. Such permission should routinely be granted *except* when the body or a major organ is to be donated. Autopsy is often very helpful in improving the knowledge and experience of doctors and in some cases is more valuable than bequeathal. Sometimes it directly benefits the family. Temporal bones;

pituitary glands; and sometimes corneas, skin, and bone can be retrieved after an autopsy.

Eyeglasses

Eyeglasses and cases (and brown artificial eyes) left by the dead (or no longer needed by the living) can be sent to New Eyes for the Needy. They have helped over three million people in the United States and other countries since their founding in 1932. In Canada, used eyeglasses are collected and distributed by Operation Eyesight Universal. See Appendix 8, "Anatomical Gifts."

Anatomical Gift Legislation

This is a controversial issue.

To encourage anatomical gifts, most American states have, since 1985, adopted laws requiring medical personnel to ask relatives at time of death if organs or tissues may be transplanted to persons in need of them ("required request"). A related measure that is gaining favor in Canada is to require doctors to indicate on the hospital chart that organ donation was considered at the time of death, and if not done, why not. Also in Canada, coroners are increasingly mandated to ask about organ donation in their inquiries following sudden or unexpected deaths. An overwhelming majority of families promptly agree, and it appears a significant increase in donations is resulting.

Going one step beyond this, Finland, Greece, Italy, Norway, Spain, and Sweden permit the removal of organs or tissues unless the patient or family expressly objects. Going further still, Austria, Poland, Denmark, Switzerland, and France permit such removal regardless of the wishes of the family. In practice, however, doctors won't do it without family permission.

Clearly, these legislative developments will go a long way toward reducing the waste of urgently needed organs and tissues.

Cost of Transplants

Organs for transplant cannot be bought, but the cost of transplantation is often high. Increasingly, these costs are being covered by Medicare, Medicaid, Canada's National Health program, and private health insurance companies. Medicaid coverage varies from state to state and from province to province, and private insurance from one company to another. Before buying health insurance, check with the company on this matter.

The Gift of Life

Resolution of the problems of anatomical gifts and education concerning their desirability will make possible the saving of thousands of lives, cure a vast amount of blindness, and relieve much suffering. Consider what it might mean to you. *You* need an organ transplant to save your life. You get one at once. *Your wife* needs a corneal transplant to restore her sight. She gets one immediately. *Your child* needs bone marrow transplants. He or she receives them. Shortages of organs and tissues could be virtually ended. This gives a wholly new and creative dimension to the human experience of death.

ENDNOTES

[1]Used by permission of Robert Test.

[2]American Council on Transplantation and United Network of Organ Sharing (UNOS).

The Living Bank International is an international registry for persons wishing to donate organs or tissues at time of death. If death is imminent or has occurred the Living Bank will refer the situation to the closest appropriate agency. To obtain a registration form, contact the Living Bank at P.O. Box 6725, Houston, TX 77265. Phone 800/528-2971 or 713/961-9431. Fax 713/961-0979. Email *info@livingbank.org*. Web *www.livingbank.org*.

Many years ago, when we were discussing a man who was being kept alive artificially after any prospect of a useful or satisfying life was past, my mother remarked, "If you let that happen to me, I'll come back and haunt you!"

When, at age ninety-five, she was in a nursing home, bedridden, almost blind and deaf, and unable to speak coherently, my father came to visit her each afternoon and to give her supper. There was much warmth and tenderness between them, and this continued to give meaning to her life.

At length, as her condition deteriorated, she decided that she had gone far enough. Her only recourse was to decline food. The nursing home responded with force-feeding—a brutal process. My father protested. "Offer her food," he said. "Give her every consideration, but do *not* force her!" When they ignored his wishes, he brought them a copy of an article Mother had written years before, arguing that a person should be free to end his or her life when his or her physical condition becomes hopeless.[1] Still they persisted, so my father and brother and I jointly called the doctor, saying, "Get the feeding stopped or get her out of there!" This time they stopped, and a few days later Mother died in peace.

I took the death certificate to the county health office while my brother fetched a box from the Friends burial committee. When we arrived to claim the body, the woman in charge exclaimed she had never heard of such a thing. She had called a funeral director who arrived the same time we did. The funeral director graciously turned to the woman in charge and said, "They know what they're doing," then bowed himself out.

We lifted Mother's body into the box and I took it home in my station wagon. In the morning, my daughter-in-law and I took her body to the medical school as she had requested. Mother had been firm about this. She was a biologist and thrifty, too. She had said she "didn't want her body wasted." The medical school would have paid for transportation but this was something I could do for her, a meaningful privilege. At the medical school we lifted Mother's body out of the box, which we took back for future use.

That afternoon my niece was being married in a nearby city. We all went. The ceremony was of a Quaker type in which there is no presiding minister, the speaking being done by the principals and others who felt moved to speak. This ceremony became a joint celebration of my mother's life and her granddaughter's marriage and was a deeply moving occasion. My father spoke of the "almost unbearable joy" that he felt in the sense of continuity. The next evening we held a memorial meeting in the community where Mother had spent most of her life. Family and friends shared their thoughts and memories and extended fellowship and support to one another. That, too, was a memorable occasion that helped to deepen the quality of our lives.

After a few months Mother's ashes were returned, in care of Vicki, my daughter-in-law, who was chairperson of the burial committee of the Friends meeting. Shortly after, our family gathered to bury those ashes at the base of the eighty-ton boulder at Antioch, which was designated as a monument to Arthur and Lucy.

A few weeks later there was another development. Vicki received from the medical school another canister of ashes, also purporting to be Lucy's ashes. "What'll we do?" asks Vicki. After some reflection I said, "Just put them in the closet." This was done, and we mentioned it to no one.

Years passed and finally Arthur Morgan, too, died at age ninety-seven. Like Lucy, he left his body to the medical school, and as with Lucy's body, I elected to take it to the medical school myself, with Vicki's help. A series of memorial gatherings were held in Yellow Springs, but the main event was a two-day convocation that was held in his memory seven months later, when his ashes would be returned from the medical school. In due time the convocation was held, and people came from far and wide to celebrate his life in a series of events.

One of these events was a ceremony in which his ashes were interred at the base of the boulder. This event was presided over by Donald Harrington, of the Community Church of New York, who had been a student at Antioch during the Morgan era.

In preparation for this event I had taken the canister of Arthur's ashes and the canister with Lucy's "duplicate" ashes and had sealed them together in a small carton. At the appropriate moment, this carton was placed in a hole at the base of the boulder by two of Arthur's great-grandchildren. No one but Lee and Vicki and I knew that there were two sets of ashes in that carton. As the hole was being filled, Lee remarked to me that it was the only way he could think of "to get Granther to sleep with another woman." How true!

In a more serious vein, I reflected that Lucy and Arthur were deeply concerned for humanity and that for an Unknown Human (like the Unknown Soldier!) to share their last resting place seemed eminently fitting.

ENDNOTE

[1]"On Drinking the Hemlock," by Lucy G. Morgan. Written in 1927, it was printed in the Dec. 1971 issue of *The Hastings Center Report.*

APPENDIX 1 / *Sources of Books, Pamphlets, and Videos*

There are hundreds of books—many of them excellent—covering all aspects of death, dying, comfort, and hope. Some of the best have been listed in the short bibliographies at the ends of individual chapters. Many can be found at a good local book store. However, there are also two sources of books and other resources that should be mentioned here.

COMPASSION BOOKS

Contact at: 477 Hannah Branch Road, Burnsville, NC 28714; 828-675-9670; fax 828-675-9687. This is the world's leading source of books on death, dying and grief (over 400 titles). Most of the titles listed at the ends of chapters in this book can be found here. They also offer a good selection of videos, and a variety of booklets suitable for giving and caring. They describe their offerings as follows:

> Resources for schools, hospitals, libraries, health care workers, individuals, children, adults, teens, counselors, churches, hospices . . . . Because . . . when sorrows are shared, validated, and experienced, people can connect in deeper, more meaningful ways.

Classifications include: For and About Children; Young People Facing Serious Illness; For and About Adolescents; Comfort for Bereaved Adults; The Art of Grieving; Professional Resources; Bereaved Parents; Childbearing and Infant Loss; Conscious Living and Dying; Music and Art to Assist Healing; Hospice—Caring for the Dying; Rituals for Remembering; Video Resources; AIDS and HIV Positive; Suicide.

FUNERAL CONSUMERS ALLIANCE

Contact at: P.O. Box 10, Hinesburg, VT 05461; 1-800-765-0107, *http://www.funerals.org.* In addition to being the principal consumer organization for those dealing with the funeral industry, FCA makes available some of the most important books on death and dying. They charge regular prices for non-members, but also offer deep discounts for those who are members of local funeral consumer organizations. If there is no local group in your area, you can support the organization by joining the national Friends of FAMSA~FCA, and often get back the full cost of membership in the savings on books and other materials alone.

Some of the materials offered are published by FCA itself. A well-known example is the *Before I Go, You Should Know* kit. This is an attractive booklet (illustrated by Edward Gorey) that you fill in, with directions and information that will be needed by survivors when you die. It comes with a freezer pouch—the idea being that the freezer is a good place to store it to be sure it is not misplaced. And there is a refrigerator magnet with a Gorey illustration reminding people that there are "Matters of Life and Death Inside."

Other FCA publications include a highly informative quarterly newsletter, a handbook for organization a funeral consumer organization, and a long list of brochures explaining such subjects as cremation, funeral planning, body donation, earth burial, and other subjects.

The organization also offers a number of other books, videos, and other resources. Examples include Lisa Carlson's *Caring for the Dead: Your Final Act of Love,* Jessica Mitford's *The American Way of Death Revisited,* and a video that demonstrates embalming methods (produced for mortuary schools, but anybody who sees it is likely to decide against embalming!). The offerings even include works with insightful humor, such as a book by cartoonist Gary Larson and a video by the old Nichols and May comedy team. An up-to-date listing can be found on the FAMSA~FCA Web site, *http://www.funerals.org.*

Alzheimer's Association, 919 N. Michigan Ave., Suite 1000, Chicago, IL 60611-1176; 312-335-8700. Has over 200 chapters and 1,600 support groups. Research, education, support, public policy, family services. Newsletter and literature.

American Association of Retired Persons (AARP) offers free product reports on many issues. The following reports pertain to issues discussed in this book: "Funerals and Burials: Goods and Services" (pub. no. D13496); "Living Trusts and Wills" (pub. no. D14535); "Prepaying Your Funeral?" (pub. no. D13188). These can be ordered by sending a postcard, with the publication numbers, to: AARP Fulfillment, 601 E Street, NW, Washington, DC 20049. Allow six to eight weeks for delivery.

American Association of Suicidology, Dept. of Health, 2459 S. Ash, Denver, CO 80222; 303-692-0985. Educational programs and publications to advance the study of suicide prevention and life-threatening behavior.

American Cancer Society, 1599 Clifton Rd., NE, Atlanta, GA 30329. Has 58 divisions and over 3,000 local groups; sponsors self-help support groups and other services for cancer patients and their families. National programs of research and education.

Americans for Death with Dignity, P.O. Box 11001, Glendale, CA 91226. Working to pass the Humane and Dignified Death Act, giving terminally ill patients the right to request a physician to aid their dying through an overdose of drugs.

Association for Death Education and Counseling, 638 Prospect Ave., Hartford, CT 06105; 860-586-7503. For death education teachers and counselors in United States and Canada. Their $115 annual membership fee includes newsletter, discounts on *Death Studies,* and *Omega: Journal on Death and Dying.*

BioFab, LLC, PO Box 990556, Redding, CA 96099; *biofab@ricestraw.com.* Manufactures strawboard coffins.

Cemetery Consumer Service Council, P.O. Box 3574, Washington, DC 20007; 703-379-6426. Industry-sponsored agency to respond to consumer complaints. Assists state cemetery boards and trade associations to establish guidelines and standards; forwards and, if necessary, mediates consumer complaints.

Centering Corporation, 1531 N. Saddle Creek Rd., Omaha, NE 68104-5064; 402-553-1200. Nonprofit and tax exempt, it provides workshops, newsletter, videos, and booklets for children and for siblings and parents bereaved through miscarriage, newborn death, death of older children or grandparents, as well as for those experiencing the death of a spouse. Highly recommended.

Choice in Dying, Inc., *See Partnership in Caring.* Long the nation's largest provider of information, education, and counseling about advance directives, Choice in Dying is changing its name while expanding its role.

The Compassionate Friends, P.O. Box 3696; Oak Brook, IL 60522-3696; 630-990-0010; fax 630-990-0246; *www.compassionatefriends.org.* A national self-help organization for bereaved parents. Has material also for bereaved siblings. Has 620 chapters. Annual conference.

Continental Association of Funeral and Memorial Societies. This is an older name for Funeral Consumers Alliance.

Credit Union National Association (CUNA), 5910 Mineral Point Rd., Madison, WI 53701; 800-937-2644. Contact for address of nearest credit union.

Cremation Association of North America, 401 N. Michigan Ave., Chicago, IL 60611; 312-644-6610. Industry trade association. Offers brochures on cremation and memorialization.

Euthanasia Research and Guidance Association (ERGO), 24892 Norris Lane, Junction City, OR 97448-9559; voice & fax 541-998-1873 (e-mail ergo@efa.org). Member of the World Federation of Right to Die Societies. "Doing groundwork for compassionate and just implementation of the right to choose to die in America."

Eye Banks. See eye and tissue bank listings, Appendix 8.

Federal Trade Commission, Funeral Rule Office. Washington, D.C. 20880; 202-376-2891.

Foundation for Hospice and Home Care, 519 C Street, N.E., Stanton Park, Washington, DC 20002; 202-547-6586. Research and educational materials and programs for advancement of care for the disadvantaged, disabled, debilitated, and aged, through alternatives to institutional care.

Foundation of Thanatology, 630 W. 168th St., New York, NY 10032; 212-928-2066. Quarterly newsletter. Extensive library; symposia on psychological aspects of death and dying. Scientific and theoretical emphasis. Offer book catalog.

Funeral Consumers Alliance, PO Box 10, Hinesburg, VT 05461; 800-765-0107; *www.funerals.org.* See Appendix 6, "Directory of Funeral Consumer Organizations."

Funeral Service Consumer Assistance Program, carried on by the National Research and Information Center, P.O. Box 276413, Milwaukee, WI 53227-0641; 800-328-6545. This agency succeeded THANACAP, which was a program of the National Funeral Directors Association.

The Grief Education Program, Mental Health Association of Colorado, Inc., 6795 E. Tennessee Ave., Suite 425, Denver, CO 80224; 303-377-3040; fax 303-377-4920. Offers support groups for bereaved; education programs on grief resolution. Training manual available; Bereavement Support Groups; Leadership Manual. Prepaid, $25.

The Hastings Center, Route 9D, Garrison, NY 10524; 914-782-8500. Publishes bimonthly *Hastings Center Report*, articles, book reviews, and annual annotated bibliographies, and holds conferences on biomedical ethics.

The Hemlock Society, P.O. Box 10810, Denver, CO 80250-1810; 800-247-7421; fax 303-639-1224. Provides information and support for the right of self-deliverance for terminally ill, mentally competent adults. Member of the World Federation of Right to Die Societies.

Hospice of Marin, 150 Nellen Ave., Corte Madera, CA 94925; 415-927-2273. Local hospice with strong national outreach for information and training.

Hospice Organizations. (See Hospice Organizations, Appendix 3)

International Association for Widowed People, P.O. Box 3564, Springfield, IL 62708. Offers services to widowed people and support groups in developing programs and activities for widowed people. Quarterly newsletter and *Survivors International* magazine. Also seminars and conferences for widowed people.

Minnesota Coalition for Death Education and Support, P.O. Box 6799, St. Paul, MN 55106; 612-779-4397. Bibliographics, speakers, information on local resources, educational programs. Newsletter, $15 a year.

National AIDS Hotline, Centers for Disease Control, Public Health Service. 800- 342-HELP.

National AIDS Information Clearing House, P.O. Box 6003, Rockville, MD 20850; 800-458-5231. General information, AIDS in the workplace, and information on clinical trials currently under way.

National Anatomical Service, 28 Eltingville Blvd., Staten Island, NY 10312; 718- 948-2400; fax 718-356-0454. A burial and cremation center offering low-cost cremation and burial services, from $695 for complete services in metropolitan New York area. Cost is $895 nationwide.

National Association for Widowed People, P.O. Box 3564, Springfield, IL 62708. Has 23,000 local groups, newsletter, and quarterly periodical.

National Funeral Directors Association (NFDA), 11121 W. Oklahoma Ave., Milwaukee, WI 53227; 414-541-2500. Leading trade association. Provides literature, audiovisual materials, and speakers on many aspects of bereavement and funeral planning.

National Hospice Organization. See Appendix 3, "Hospice Organizations."

National Institute on Drug Abuse, Drug Information & Treatment Hotline 9 A.M. to 3 P.M. EST Mon.–Fri.; 12 noon to 3 P.M. EST Sat. & Sun. 800-662-HELP.

National Self-Help Clearing House, Graduate School and University Center, City University of New York, 25 West 43rd Street, Room 620, New York, NY 10036; 212-354-8525. Provides information on peer support groups of all kinds, and how to organize them.

Partnership for Caring, 1035 30th Street NW, Washington, DC 20007; 1-800-989-9455, 202-338-9790; fax 202-338-0242; *www.partnershipforcaring.org*. This is the successor organization to Choice in Dying, which invented living wills in 1967 and has long been a leading supplier of information on end-of-life issues. Partnership for Caring is devoted to raising consumer expectations and increasing demand for excellent end-of-life care.

Parents of Murdered Children, Inc., 100 E. 8th St., Rm. B-41, Cincinnati, OH 45202. Founded by parent survivors in 1978 for parents and other survivors of murder victims. Provides information, advocacy, and newsletter to meet the unique needs of murder survivors. Local support groups.

Pregnancy and Infant Loss Center, 1421 E. Wayzata Blvd., Suite 30, Wayzata, MN 55391; 612-473-9372. Support, referral, resources, and education after miscarriage, stillbirth, and newborn death.

Seasons: Suicide Bereavement, P.O. Box 187, Park City, UT 84060. Information and referral for survivor-victims of suicide. Local support groups.

SHARE–Pregnancy & Infant Loss Support National Office, St. Joseph Health Center, 300 First Capitol Dr., St. Charles, MO 63301; 800-821-6819. Founding group for infant-death support groups.

St. Mary's Grief Support Center, 407 East 3rd St., Duluth, MN 55805-4402; 218-726-4402. Conducts specialized support groups for children, youth, adults, siblings, parents, infertile couples. Provides literature and useful prototypes.

St. Francis Center, 4880A MacArthur Blvd., N.W., Washington, DC 20007; 202- 333-4880; fax 202-333-4540. Nonsectarian organization providing professional counseling, education and training, and volunteer support to individuals and organizations facing life-threatening illness and bereavement. Publishes quarterly journal, *Centering* for membership and *Living with* AIDS*: Perspectives for Caregivers,* a training manual for caregivers. Annual workshop series for health and mental health professionals, school personnel, and community on psychosocial issues of illness and grief.

Suicide Prevention Center, Inc., P.O. Box 1393, Dayton, OH 45401-1393. Provides pamphlets, manuals, audiovisuals, including after a suicide death. Business office: 937-297-9096, Crisis line: 937-297-4777.

TLC Group, P.O. Box 28551, Dallas, TX 75228; 972-681-5303; fax 972-681-5445 (e-mail: *tlc@metronet.com*; URL: *http://www.metronet.com-tlc*). Excellent list of books for health professionals and others. Send for free booklist, or call for information.

Widowed Persons Service, American Association of Retired Persons, 601 E Street, NW, Washington, DC 20049; 202-434-2260. Provides assistance in developing local support programs for widowed people, public education about needs of the widowed and services available, directory of services for widowed persons. Free pamphlet: "On Being Alone." There are over 240 local AARP Widowed Persons Service programs in which trained volunteers reach out to newly widowed persons. For a program near you call 800-424-3410.

National Hospice Organization. 1901 N. Moore St., Suite 901, Arlington, VA 22209; 703-243-5900, or Hospice Help Line: 800-658-8898. NHO is the national coordinating body for hospice organizations. It sponsors national and regional meetings, develops standards of care, provides education materials and newsletter, and advocates for hospice to government and private insurance programs. A call on the Hospice Help Line can get the name and address of the nearest hospice.

Hospice Education Institute. 190 Westbrook Rd., Essex, CT 06426-0713; Call Hospice Link: 800-331-1620; in Connecticut and Alaska call 203-767-1620. Through their computerized "Hospicelink," HEI refers callers immediately to the nearest hospice. Also coordinates regional, national, and international seminars and training for hospice professionals, health care providers, and civic groups; presents community education programs; consultation to existing hospice programs and to groups seeking to begin hospice care.

Children's Hospice International. 2202 Mt. Vernon Ave., Alexandria, VA 22301; 800-242-4453, Mon. & Wed. 9–4. Assists parents and health education workers with material dealing with children with life-threatening illness.

FINANCIAL HELP FOR TERMINAL CARE

Medicare. This is an insurance program administered by the Social Security System for recipients of Social Security payments. Medicare A covers some home health services provided by a state-certified home health agency, if a patient is homebound, in need of skilled nursing service, and under a doctor's plan of treatment. Covered services may include skilled nursing, home health aids, medical equipment and supplies, and medical social work. There is co-payment of twenty percent for equipment and appliances.

Since 1983, Medicare has also provided an optional hospice benefit for eligible patients who are certified as having less than six months to live. A person who signs up for the hospice benefit automatically waives Medicare A coverage for the terminal illness while under the care of hospice. Covered services may include physical and occupational therapy, speech therapy, homemaker services, medical supplies, physician's services, short-term inpatient care, respite care for the family, and counseling, including bereavement counseling. Services must be provided by a federally certified hospice, meeting Medicare's standards for scope of services, written plans for patient care, and centralized recordkeeping and administration. Benefits are paid according to a set daily rate, and need not be separately authorized.

Because of the rigorous standards for certification, many smaller hospices have not applied for certification and therefore are not eligible for Medicare payment. There is concern that as hospice becomes an institutionalized part of our health care system, it may tend to lose its former spirit of volunteerism, enthusiasm, and flexibility in meeting the needs of patients, families, and communities.

Medicaid. This is a state-supervised, county-administered program whose benefits and requirements vary from state to state. If your income is near the poverty level and you own no more than your house, car, and minimal savings, you may be eligible. Your county social services agency can tell you the requirements and determine your eligibility. Medicaid generally has a deductible amount ("spend-down") after which it covers one hundred percent of such expenses as medicines, skilled nursing, doctor's visits, medical supplies, and appliances. This program is especially important for those under sixty-five who do not quality for Medicare.

Private Insurance. Many insurance policies cover some home health care services, even without specific hospice benefits, and increasingly, companies are including a provision for hospice coverage as part of standard benefits or as supplemental coverage offered separately. Counseling and bereavement services are not normally included. When a hospice program is not certified, a company will make its own assessment to decide about reimbursing the provider agency. Companies are more likely to cover home care if it can be demonstrated that this will enable them to save hospital costs. Inquire of individual companies, preferably in advance of need, to determine the specific benefits they offer.

Other Assistance. Housekeeper or chore services, home health aides, health appliances, and other support services may be available from other sources. Senior citizen programs, private social service agencies, and private health-related organizations offer a variety of help to those eligible. Hospital, health department, and hospice social workers, and community information-and-referral services can provide leads. It is sometimes surprising what services can be discovered if one is persistent and keeps asking for suggestions.

Tips on Dealing with Bureaucracies. Always make a note of the date of any conversation, the person you spoke with, and the substance of what was said. Keep an orderly file of all written communication. If delays or contradictions arise, this will make it much easier to check back on your understanding and resolve the problem. If delay or confusion persists, don't hesitate to ask for a resolution from a supervisor. In most offices there is someone you can talk to as one human being to another. Keep going until you find that person.

Some local and many state governments have telephone numbers that citizens may call to obtain accurate information about government programs. Local employees may be confused by frequent changes in regulations. Also, you can ask a hospital or health-department social worker, or a citizen advocacy group.

A living will declaration is a document instructing one's doctor and family to refrain from measures to prolong the process of dying when one is terminally ill and unable to communicate one's wishes. A health care agent is a person you designate to make health-care decisions for you if you cannot express them yourself. Both are important if, for example, you want to receive comfort-care only after there is no hope of recovery or resumption of a reasonable quality of life.

Forty-six states and the District of Columbia have adopted legislation that recognize both living wills and the right to designate a health care agent. Therefore, it is easier to list the exceptions than to list the states with both of these protections. One state—Alaska—authorizes living wills, but not health care agents. Three states—Massachusetts, Michigan, and New York— authorize appointment of health care agents, but not living wills. Again, every other state authorizes both.

Detailed information on these issues, and on the laws of each state, may be obtained from Choice in Dying, Inc., 475 Riverside Drive, Room 1852, New York, NY 10115; 212-870-2003; Web site *http://www.choices.org*, fax 212-870-2040;

As of this writing, late in the year 2000, Choice in Dying is gradually merging with another organization, Partnership for Caring. Its Web site is *http://www.partnershipforcaring.org.*

Living Will Declaration

Following is the Living Will Declaration that Choice in Dying, Inc., recommends when no state form is provided:

> To My Family, Doctors, and All Those Concerned with My Care:
> I, _____, being of sound mind, make this statement as a directive to be followed if I become unable to participate in decisions regarding my medical care.
> If I should be in an incurable or irreversible mental or physical condition with no reasonable expectation of recovery, I direct my attending physician to withhold or withdraw treatment that merely

prolongs my dying. I further direct that treatment be limited to measures to keep me comfortable and to relieve pain.

These directions express my legal right to refuse treatment. Therefore I expect my family, doctors, and everyone concerned with my care to regard themselves as legally and morally bound to act in accord with my wishes, and in so doing to be free of any legal liability for having followed my directions.

I especially do not want:

[enumerate]

Other Instructions/comments:

[list them]

Proxy Designation Clause: Should I become unable to communicate my instructions as stated above, I designate the following person to act in my behalf:

[Give name and address]

If the person I have named above is unable to act in my behalf, I authorize the following person to do so:

[Give name and address]

Signed:_____Date:_____

Witness:_____Witness:_____

(Keep the signed original with your personal papers at home. Give signed copies to doctors, family, and proxy. Review your declaration from time to time; initial and date it to show it still expresses your intent.)

An Alternative Living Will

This form was drafted and signed by Ernest Morgan and endorsed in writing by his family and physician:

I want to have some control over my own death. In the event of *any* illness I want to know whether any given treatment is for recovery or life support, or whether it is for comfort. And I want to be free to accept or decline any specific treatment. In the event of my incapacity to make such decisions, because of unconsciousness or other condition, for more than 24 hours, that circumstance shall constitute a decision against treatment directed toward recovery or life support.

When death does come I want to go as gracefully and comfortably as possible, and not be held back by well-meaning medics and family.

[Add Organ Donor Provision, below, if desired.]

Signed:_____Date:_____

We accept and support Ernest's perspective in this matter.

[Signed by wife, children, and personal physician]

(The above document is appropriate to persons over sixty-five. For younger persons, a longer period should be specified.)

Additional Provision for Organ Donors

However, I have bequeathed organs of my body for medical purposes. Therefore, if my body is brain dead, I wish and authorize the use of organ/tissue–support procedures, but at no expense to my survivors or my estate, to keep those tissues alive until a qualified surgical team can remove them.

Statement to Accompany Donated Organs

I am attaching the following statement, signed only "The Donor and family" to my living will and whatever other documents will give it the best chance of coming into the hands of person(s) receiving organs or tissues from my body.

I am pleased with the prospect that organs or tissues from my body may, after my death, find service in the life of another. This symbolizes, in a tangible way, the unity of life.

To you, the recipient, I offer gratitude for making me a participant in your life and for helping add a creative dimension to my death. May you enjoy health and happiness.

—The Donor and family

BURIAL BOXES

Repeatedly people have asked where to buy, or how to build, simple burial boxes. The following information is intended primarily for families or groups who wish to carry out their own arrangements without a funeral director. While funeral directors ordinarily provide a casket, many will work with homemade burial boxes if requested.

Multipurpose Boxes: Sometimes people buy or build nicely handcrafted boxes in advance of need to use as furniture: a settee, linen chest, or cabinet (by standing it on end with shelves inserted).

Corrugated Fiber Boxes: These can be made by any firm that makes fiber boxes, but their minimum order is generally large. Many crematories and funeral directors can provide one at a cost of from $15 to $125.

SIZES OF BURIAL BOXES	¾" Plywood Cheap Grade		¼" Plywood Cheap Grade		¾" Lumber or Plywood
	Bottom (1 needed)	Ends (2 needed)	Sides (2 needed)	Top (1needed)	Side Strips (2 needed)
LARGE SIZE Outside 6'6"x26"x16" Inside 6'4½"x24"x15"	6'4½" x 25½"	26" x 15¾"	6'4½" x 15¾"	6'6" x 26"	6'4½" x 5"
MEDIUM SIZE Outside 6'x21"x13½" Inside 5"10½"x19"x12½"	5'10½" x 20½"	21" x 13¼"	5'10½" x 13¼	6' x 21"	5'10½" x 5"
SMALL SIZE Outside 5'6"x21"x13½" Inside 5'4½"x19"x12½"	5'4½" x 20½"	21" x 13¼"	5'4½" x 13¼"	5"6" x 21"	5'4½" x 4"
CHILD SIZE Outside 3'11"x16"x11" Inside 3'9½"x14"x10"	3'9½" x 15½"	16" x 10¾"	3'9½" x 10¾"	3'11" x 16"	3'9½" x 3"

Inexpensive Plywood Boxes: We offer here instructions for making four sizes of plywood boxes, which are inexpensive, compact, and easy to build. The burial committee of Celo Friends Meeting, for example, keeps on hand a set of wooden parts for all four sizes of burial box, which can be quickly assembled when needed. These boxes are not suitable for body transportation by common carrier or for keeping an unembalmed body for any length of time. If used at a funeral, they may be placed on a low bench or other support and covered by a cloth (pall).

Homemade Burial Boxes

Instructions: These four boxes can be made from 2 sheets of ¾" plywood and 3½ sheets of ¼" plywood. Anyone modestly experienced with tools can assemble the boxes.

Chart for Cutting Plywood Sheets: Two sheets of ¾" 4'×8' plywood, cut as shown in the two diagrams below, will provide all the ¾" plywood parts needed to build the four sizes of boxes. The ¼" plywood is simpler and needs no cutting chart, so we have simply explained below how it should be cut.

Cutting instructions for ¼" plywood: (No diagrams needed)

First Sheet (4'×8'): Top for Large Size box (6'6"×26"), and one side (6'4½"×15¾"). Cut long way.

Top for Child Size (3'11"×16"). Cut from remaining end.

Second Sheet: Top for Medium Size (6'×21"), and two sides (5'10½"×13¾"). Cut long way.

Two sides for Child Size (3'9½"×10¾"). Cut from end piece.

Third Sheet: Top for Small Size (5'6"×21"), and two sides (5'4½"×13¼"). Cut long way.

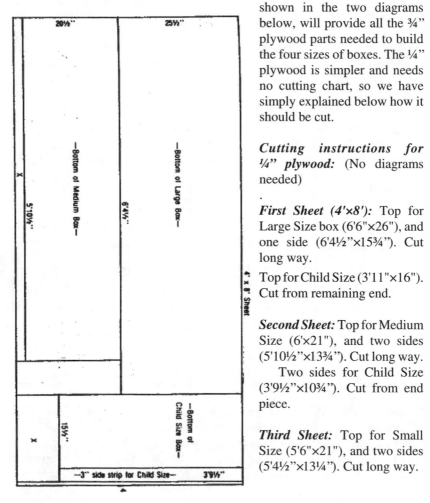

1ˢᵗ Sheet of ¾" Plywood

A large end piece will be left over. This can be used to make an extra top and side of Child Size for possible future use.

Still Needed: The second side for the Large Size. If the lumber yard has part of a sheet from which this can be cut, fine. If not, a fourth sheet will be needed. In that case, the rest of the sheet can be cut into spare parts and stored with the boxes for possible later use.

Also Needed: Two side strips of ¾" lumber for Large Size (5"×6'4½").

Two side strips of ¾" lumber for Medium Size (5"×5'10½").

Two side strips of ¾" lumber for Small Size (4"×5'4½").

(Side strips for Child Size were included in a previous cut.)

From the hardware store, get some 7/8" nails, and some 4- and 8-penny box nails and four chest handles for each box. The handles should be of a kind that hang down when not in use and stay in horizontal position when lifted. Don't forget to get screws for these.

Assembly Instructions

Nail a narrow strip to each side piece, flush with the edge and the end, using 4-penny nails. The good side of the plywood should be out.

Nail the side pieces to the bottom, using 7/8" nails. The strips should be inside and at the top.

Nail the ends, with the good sides out, firmly to the bottom and to the side strips, using 8-penny nails, and the job is done.

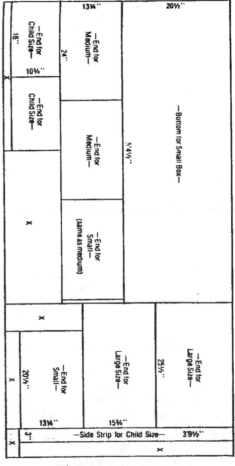

2ⁿᵈ Sheet of 3/4" Plywood

The handles may be stored inside the box and screwed on when the box is used. Likewise, the cover may be tacked lightly in place until the box is needed, and then nailed firmly down with 7/8" nails when the box is used.

CAUTION: The box, when loaded, should be moved with care to avoid pulling the ends away from the box. After the cover has been nailed down, however, the box is quite strong and can be handled freely. By using screws in the ends instead of nails, the box can be made quite strong without the lid.

Assembly Diagram

When the box is used, two handles should be screwed to each end for ease in going through doors. They may be removed with a screwdriver and brought home from the crematory or cemetery for future use.

When a body is taken to the medical school in one of these boxes, it is customary to remove the body from the box and take the box home.

To save storage space, these boxes are so designed that the medium size can nest inside the large size, and the child size inside the small size.

The design for these boxes is based, with modifications, on ones used for years by the burial committee of the Yellow Springs Friends Meeting. They are sturdy, inexpensive, easy to build, and compact to store. Since they have been modified from the original design, we will appreciate comments and criticism from anyone who uses this design.

Burial Forms

At the end of this appendix is a copy of the form developed by the Burial Committee of the Yellow Springs (Ohio) Friends Meeting. It has been in use, virtually unchanged, for thirty years. (Their term *burial* in this case is figurative. In practice, the committee was concerned only with cremation or removal to a medical school.)

Each family wishing to be served by the committee was required to fill out a Registration of Intent for each member of the family, presumably *in advance* of need. This was done in duplicate, one copy being filed by the committee, the other retained by the family.

Very importantly, each family was expected to clear their plans in advance with all close relatives. Failure to do this commonly resulted in painful misunderstandings at the time of death.

About every five years the committee would review all the forms on file, to bring them up to date. The first time, this was done by mailing the forms to the families, asking them to update and return them. People don't like to think about death, however—especially their own—and they put off reviewing the forms, with the result that many were not returned. After that, the committee decided to update the forms by phone calls or personal visits.

A Few Words of Counsel

Many churches and individual clergymen receive substantial support and gifts from morticians and as a result are reluctant to protect their parishioners from exploitative funeral prices or provide them with comparative price lists. Some clergymen even ask morticians for kickbacks or high clergy fees for their services.

Morticians are required by law to give price information over the phone to anyone who calls, and to give visitors to the mortuary a copy of their general price list to keep, and to show them their casket price list. Cooperative firms will allow visitors to keep the casket price list. Among the most frequently overpriced items are caskets. A casket costing the mortician $200 may be sold to a customer for $400, $800, or even $1,200, often depending on how much the mortician thinks the customer will be able to scrape together. In asking the price of a casket it is often helpful to ask for the manufacturer's name and manufacturer's model number (some mortuaries make up their own to confuse customers).

If a mortician refuses to give this information, you may call the Federal Trade Commission's (FTC) Funeral Rule office in Washington, D.C. Their number is 202-376-2891. They encourage people to call them. The FTC will in turn contact the mortician to obtain the information and advise him to cooperate. Simply telling a mortician that you will call the FTC if necessary may be sufficient to obtain the appropriate information.

Newspapers, broadcasting stations, churches, and groups interested in making a survey of local funeral costs and practices may contact a local funeral information society or the national FCA office for advice and information.

A number of methods designed to pressure lower-priced mortuaries into charging high prices or go out of business, mislead and bribe the clergy, and exploit consumers have appeared or have increased in recent years.

Two of the most harmful methods are those of large chains and high-priced mortuaries which:

— have taken over a majority, or all, seats on state funeral boards (which should be composed mostly or totally of consumers in order to protect the public) and then harassing lower-priced mortuaries or making regulations to cripple them in order to force them to raise their prices or go out of business (such as requiring that anyone who talks to customers must be a licensed embalmer or "funeral director," making it difficult for nonembalmers to own or operate mortuaries, although most mortuaries need an embalmer for only a few hours a week, and can hire one for those few hours);

— are providing trips, pagers, and substantial gifts to clergymen to coax the clergy to recommend these mortuaries to their people, not object to unfair high prices being charged, not object to the heavy-handed treatment of lower-priced mortuaries by the stacked state funeral boards, and not survey local mortuaries' prices and provide comparative price lists to their parishioners to assist them to protect themselves from overcharges;

—and have salespersons who:
- — pressure customers,
- — make verbal statements and promises which are contrary to what is in the contract; and
- — write inadequate or false descriptions of services or merchandise on the contracts (even writing model numbers of lower-priced items than people are paying for), meaning that customers will not receive the services or goods they thought they were buying.

Other developments include:

1. Large chains have bought up mortuaries, cemeteries, and flower shops in many communities across the country, and in many cases have increased the previous prices by double or more with no visible change in service.
2. Many prepayment plans charge outrageously high prices for services and merchandise, and use contracts with harmful terms such as:
   - — *nontransferable* if a person moves to another location;
   - — *nonrefundable,* meaning no refund if a person needs to cancel even after making most of the payment;
   - — *cancelable by the plan or mortuary, with no refund* if the buyer cannot make a payment on time;
   - — *noncancelable*, meaning the buyer or his estate will have to keep paying on the contract even if the funeral can never be used.

Families should not sign any contract until they compare prices and show the contract to an accountant or attorney.

REGISTRATION OF INTENT OF SIMPLE BURIAL
Yellow Springs (Ohio) Friends Meeting

THIS FORM, filled out, also includes information for obituary and legal data for death certificates.

NAME_____

Address_____

DATE FILLED OUT

County_____S.S. No._____

Date of Birth_____Place_____

DATES REVIEWED
_____
_____
_____

Father's Name_____

Mother's Maiden Name_____

I desire that, if circumstances permit at the time of my death, the Yellow Springs Monthly Meeting of Friends shall carry out the arrangements set forth below.

Date_____   Signature_____

Witness_____   Witness_____

__I wish my body cremated.

__ I wish my body given to a medical school. (See bequeathal form)

__ I wish my eyes given to an eye bank.

Disposal of Remains: Check which of the following dispositions of ashes you request:

__ Left at crematory for disposal there.

__ Delivered to one of the following:

(List names and addresses in order of preference)

Form of memorial service: Unless otherwise specified, the usual practice would be a memorial worship meeting at Rockford after the disposal of the body and with no expenditure for flowers. There will be no public viewing of the body. Please indicate any specific requests:

Next of Kin: The following information is necessary to clear the Meeting's actions immediately on death of a participant. List next of kin in order of precedence:

NAME, PERMANENT ADDRESS, AND TELEPHONE

1.

2.

3.

Do you expect full understanding and cooperation on the part of the above individuals?

A member of the Burial Committee will discuss with you the circumstances requiring any qualified answer.

Endorsements: We understand and are in accord with the intent indicated above:

NAME   DATE

_____

_____

_____

(Members of immediate family—next of kin)

FOLLOWING TO BE SIGNED AFTER DEATH OF REGISTRANT:

I authorize the Burial Committee of Yellow Springs Friends Meeting to carry out the program indicated above.

Signature:

Date:

Two Witnesses:

OVER

BIOGRAPHICAL DATA   (Suggest pencil for items subject to change)

Marital Status_____ Wedding date_____

Usual Occupation_____Business or Industry_____

Parents' Residence (if living)_____

Sisters' & Brothers' Residences_____

_____

_____

Children's Residences_____

_____

_____

Schools attended (Dates)_____

_____

When moved here_____

Organizations, community projects, special achievements_____

_____

_____

_____

_____

(The following information is required by law for the death certificate of a veteran.)

Name of war or dates of service_____

Type of Discharge_____Date_____Rank_____

Service (Army, Navy, etc.)_____

Unit (as Company, Battery, Ship, etc.)_____

Branch (Infantry, Artillery, etc.)_____
(This data may be gotten from a veteran's discharge papers.)

(OVER)

APPENDIX 6 / *Directory of Funeral Consumer Organizations*

The national office serving local Funeral Consumer Organizations throughout the U.S. is Funeral Consumer Alliance (FCA), P.O. Box 10, Hinesburg, VT 05461; 800-765-0107. Web site: *http://www.funerals.org*.

Canadian memorial societies are listed here, too. They are not united by a national organization, so each abides by its own standards and rules.

Educational Materials From FCA

The national office offers these materials at full-price for non-members, and at reduced prices for local affiliates. If you live in a location not served by a local affiliate, you may join a national group called *Friends of FCA,* and also qualify for a discount.

The selections include well-known books such as Lisa Carlson's *Caring For The Dead: Your Final Act of Love* and Jessica Mitford's *The American Way of Death Revisited.* Other publications are prepared specifically by FCA, including a quarterly newsletter and a manual for starting a local organization. A very popular item is *Before I Go, You Should Know*—an end-of-life planning kit that comes in a plastic pouch with state-specific Living Will and Durable Power of Attorney for Health Care. It is extremely attractive, with illustrations by the late Edward Gorey.

DIRECTORY OF CANADIAN MEMORIAL SOCIETIES

Alberta
Calgary: Calgary Co-op Memorial Society, 216 Marpole Bay NE T2A 4W9
403-248-2044
Edmonton: Soc. of Edmonton & District, 10242 105th St. T5S 3L5
403-944-0196
Red Deer: Memorial Society of Red Deer & District, P.O. Box 817 T4N 5H2
403-340-1021

Br. Columbia
Vancouver: Memorial Society of B.C., 212-624 Sixth St., New Westminster V3L 3C4
604-527-1012

Manitoba
Winnipeg: Funeral Planning & Mem. Society of Manitoba, c/o 661 Jubilee Ave. R3L 1P5
204-452-7999

New Brunswick
Fredericton: Mem. Society of New Brunswick (Fredericton Branch), Box 622 E3B 5A6

Ontario
Belleville: Memorial Society of Quinte, 16 Linton Park Rd. K8N 4K6
613-968-7640
Guelph: Memorial Society of Guelph, P.O. Box 1784 N1H 7A1
519-822-7430
Hamilton: Hamilton Mem. Soc., P.O. Box 89026-991 King St. W. L8S 4R5
905-389-8240
Kingston: Mem. Soc. of Kingston & District, c/o Margaret Burdsall, 960 Killarney Cr. K7M 8C6
613-531-8948
Kitchener: Mem. Society of Kitchener-Waterloo, 146 Union Blvd. N2M 2S2
519-579-3800 / (Cambridge) 653-5705

117

London: Mem. Society of London, P.O. Box 1729, Station A   N6A 5H9
519-472-0670
Niagara Falls: Niagara Peninsula Memorial Society, P.O. Box 2102, 4500 Queen St.   L2E 6Z2
905-358-5060
Ottawa: Ottawa Memorial Society, #1903-1025 Richmond Rd. K2B 8G8
613-828-4926
Peterborough: Funeral Planning Assn. (Mem. Soc.) of Peterborough & District, P.O. Box 1795   K9J 7X6
705-742-0550
Sudbury: Memorial Society of Northern Ontario, Attn: Jean Maitland, 384 Van Horne St. P3B 1J3
705-673-5532
Thunder Bay: Mem. Soc. of Thunder Bay, P.O. Box 501, Station F P7C 4W4   807-683-3051

Toronto: Funeral Advisory & Memorial Society, 55 St. Phillips Rd., Etobicoke   M9P 2N8 416-241-6274
Windsor: Memorial Soc. of Windsor District P.O. Box 481   N9A 6M6
519-969-6767 / 966-1064

Quebec

Montreal: Memorial Assn. of Montreal, P.O. Box 881   H4A 3S3
514-485-8527

Saskatchewan

Lloydminster: Lloydminster-Vermilion & District Mem. Soc., 4805 -47th St. S9V 0K2   306-825-3769
Saskatoon: Memorial Soc. of Saskatchewan, P.O. Box 1846   S7K 3S2
306-374-5190

DIRECTORY OF U. S. FUNERAL CONSUMER ORGANIZATIONS

Please note: Local organizations are, in the vast majority of cases, run by volunteers. Consequently, the phone numbers change fairly frequently, as different volunteers take over the responsibilities. If you reach an answering machine, please leave a message. If you have difficulty getting through to a local group, call the national office at 800-765-0107. If there is no local organization in your area, you may inquire about starting one, or join the national *Friends of FCA* organization.

Call the FCA office   *Alabama*

Alaska

Anchorage Cook Inlet Memorial, P.O. Box 102414, 99510   907-566-3732

Arizona

Phoenix Valley Memorial Society, P.O. Box 0423, Chandler, 85244-0423
480-929-9659
Prescott Memorial Society of Prescott, P.O. Box 1090, 86302-1090
520-778-3000
Tucson Memorial Society of So. Arizona, P.O. Box 12661, 85732-2661
520-721-0230

Arkansas

Fayetteville NW Arkansas Mem. Society, P.O. Box 3055, 72702-3055
501-582-1631
Little Rock Memorial Society of Arkansas, 11621 Hilaro Springs Rd., 72206
888-278-7556, 501-562-6361

California

Bakersfield Kern Memorial Society, P.O. Box 1202, 93302-1202
661-854-5689, 661-366-7266
Berkeley Bay Area Funeral Society, P.O. Box 264, 94701-0264   510-841-6653
Cotati Redwood Funeral Society, P.O. Box 7501, 94931-7501 707-568-7684
Eureka/Arcata Humboldt Funeral Society, P.O. Box 856, Arcata 95518
707-822-8599
Fresno Valley Memorial Society, P.O. Box 101, 93707-0101   559-268-2181
Los Angeles Los Angeles Funeral Soc., P.O. Box 92313, Pasadena 91109
626-683-3545, 683-3752
Modesto Stanislaus Memorial Society, P.O. Box 4252, 95352-4252
209-521-7690
Palo Alto Funeral & Mem. Planning Soc., P.O. Box 60448, 94306-0448
650-321-2109, 888-775-5553

Sacramento Sacramento Valley Mem. Soc., P.O. Box 161688, 95816-1688
916-451-4641

San Diego San Diego Memorial Society, 4883 Ronson Ct., Ste. L, 92111-1812
858-874-7921

San Luis Obispo Central Coast Mem. Soc., P.O. Box 679, 93406-0679
805-543-6133

Santa Barbara Fun'l Cons. Allnc./ Channel Cities, P. O. Box 1778, Ojai 93024
805-640-0109, 800-520-PLAN

Santa Cruz Fun'l & Mem. Soc. Monterey Bay, Box 2900, 95063-2900
831-426-3308

Stockton San Joaquin Memorial Society, Box 4832, 95204-4832
209-465-2741

Colorado

Denver Funeral Consumer Society of CO, 4101 E. Hampden Ave., 80222
303-759-2800, 888-438-6431

Connecticut

Bridgewater Fun'l Consumer Info Soc of CT, P.O. Box 34, 06752
(CT) 800-607-2801, 860-355-4197

Delaware

Served by Maryland Alliance

District of Columbia

Washington Mem. Soc. of Metro Washington, 1500 Harvard St. NW, 20009
202-234-7777

Florida

Cocoa Funeral Consumers Assn. Brevard Co., P.O. Box 276, 32923-0276
321-242-1421, 321-255-2100

DeBary Funeral Society of Mid-Florida, P.O. Box 392, 32713-0392
904-789-1682, 407-668-6822

Ft. Myers Funeral & Mem. Soc. of SW Fla., P.O. Box 7756, 33911-7756
941-573-0507

Gainesville Memorial Society of Alachua Co., Box 14662, 32604-4662
352-374-6671

Orlando Funeral Consumrs Alliance Orlando, P.O. Box 953, Goldenrod 32733
407-677-5009

Palm Beach Gardens Palm Beach Funeral Society, P.O. Box 31982, 33420
561-659-4881

Pensacola & Ft. Walton Beach Fun'l & Mem. Soc../Pensacola & W. Fla. 5425 Dynasty Dr., 32504
850-477-9085

Sarasota Funeral Cons. Allnc/ Sarasota-Manatee Co., P.O. Box 15833, 34277
941-953-3740

St. Petersburg Suncoast-Tampa Mem. Soc., 719 Arlington Ave. N., 33701
727-520-8922

Tallahassee Fun'l Consumers Assn Leon Co. 1006 Buena Vista Dr., 32304
850-224-2082

Tampa Funeral Consumers Assn. Tampa Bay, 18902 Arbor Dr., Lutz, 33549-5051

Georgia

Atlanta Memorial Society of Georgia, 1911 Cliff Valley Way NE, 30329
404-634-2896, 800-840-4339

Macon Middle Georgia Chapter 5276 Zebulon Rd., 31210   use the 800#

Hawaii

Honolulu Memorial Society of Hawaii, 505 Ward Ave., Suite 203, 96814
808-589-2884

Idaho

Boise Funeral Consumers Alliance of Idaho, P.O. Box 1919, 83701-1919
208-426-0032

Illinois

Chicago Chicago Memorial Association, Box 2923, 60690-2923 773-238-3746

Urbana Champaign County Mem. Society, 309 W. Green St., 61801

Indiana

Bloomington Bloomington Mem. Society, 2120 N. Fee Lane, 47408

Indianapolis Indianapolis Mem. Society, 5805 E. 56th St., 46226
317-844-1371

Valparaiso Memorial Soc. of NW Indiana, P.O. Box 329, 46384-0329
219-464-3024

Iowa

Iowa City Mem. Society of Iowa River Valley, 120 N. Dubuque St., 52245
319-338-2637

For all other areas, call the FCA office

Kansas
Check Missouri or call the FCA office

Kentucky
Louisville Mem. Soc. of Greater Louisville, P.O. Box 5326, 40255-5326
502-454-4855

Louisiana
Baton Rouge Mem. Soc. of Greater
Baton Rouge, 8470 Goodwood Ave.,
70806

Maine
Auburn Memorial Society of Maine, Box
3122, 04212-3122
800-218-9885, 207-786-4323

Maryland
Bethesda Funeral Consumers Alliance/
MD & Environs, 9601 Cedar Lane,
20814   800-564-0017

Massachusetts
Boston The Memorial Society, 66 Marl-
borough St., 02116
617-859-7990, 888-666-7990
East Orleans Funeral Cons. Allnc/Cape
Cod, P. O. Box 1375, 02643-1375
508-862-2522, 800-976-9552
New Bedford Memorial Society of SE
Mass., 71 8th St., 02740
508-996-0046
Springfield Mem Soc of Western Mass.,
P.O. Box 2821, 01101-2821
413-783-7987

Michigan
Ann Arbor Mem Advisory & Planning
Soc., 2030 Chaucer Drive, 48103
734-665-9516
Detroit Greater Detroit Memorial Soci-
ety, P.O. Box 24054, 48224-4054
313-886-0998
Flint Memorial Society of Flint, P.O.
Box 4315, 48504-4315

For all other areas, call the FCA office

Minnesota
St. Cloud Minn. Funeral & Memorial
Soc., 717 Riverside Dr. SE, 56304
320-252-7540

Call the FCA office   **Mississippi**

Missouri
Kansas City Funeral Consumer Alliance
of K. C., 4501 Walnut St., 64111
816-561-6322
St. Louis Funeral Consumer Info Soc.,
216 E. Argonne Ave., 63122-4310
314-997-9819

Montana
Billings Memorial Society of Montana,
1024 Princeton Ave., 59102
406-252-5065
Missoula Five Valleys Memorial Society,
405 University Ave. 59801

Nebraska
Call the FCA office

Nevada
Reno Funeral Consumer Info. Soc. of
NV, Box 8413, Univ. Sta.,
89507-8413   775-329-7705

New Hampshire
Epping Memorial Society of New Hampshire, P.O. Box 941, 03042-0941
603-679-5721

New Jersey
Cherry Hill Memorial Soc. of So. Jersey
401 Kings Highway N., 08034
856-235-2783
East Brunswick Raritan Valley Memorial Soc., 176 Tices Ln., 08816
732-572-1470
Lincroft Mem Assoc. of Monmouth Co. ,
1475 W. Front St., 07738
732-747-7950
Madison Morris Memorial Society, Box
509, 07940-0509   973-540-9140
Montclair Fun'l Consumers All'nc. Essex
Co., P.O. Box 1327, 07042-1327
973-783-1145
Paramus Central Memorial Society, 156
Forest, 07652   201-385-4153
Plainfield Memorial Society of Plainfield,
724 Park Ave., 07060
908-889-6289
Princeton Princeton Memorial Assoc.,
48 Roper Road, 08540 609-924-5525

New Mexico
Albuquerque Fun'l Cons. Info. Soc. No.
NM, P.O. Box 53464, 87153
505-296-5902

Las Cruces Mem. & Fun'l Soc. of So. NM, P.O. Box 6531, 88006-6531
505-526-7761

New York

Albany Mem. Soc. Hudson-Mohawk Region, 405 Washington Ave., 12206
518-465-9664

Binghamton Southern Tier Mem. Society, c/o Haeseler, 300 Fordham Rd., Vestal, 13850

Buffalo Greater Buffalo Memorial Society, 695 Elmwood Ave., 14222-1601
716-837-8636

Corning Memorial Society of Grtr Corning, 259 Delevan Ave., 14830
607-962-7132, 607-936-6563

Ithaca Ithaca Memorial Society, Box 134, 14851-0134   607-273-8316

Long Island Memorial Society of LI, P.O. Box 701, Greenlawn, 11740-0701   631-544-0383

New Hartford Mohawk Valley Mem. Soc., P. O. Box 322,13413-0322
315-797-2396, 315-735-6268

New York Mem. Soc. of Riverside Church, 490 Riverside Drive, Rm. 537, 10027   212-870-6785

New York Community Church Funeral Soc., 40 East 35th St., 10016

Poughkeepsie Mid-Hudson Memorial Soc., 249 Hooker Ave., 12603
914-229-0241

Rochester Rochester Memorial Society, 220 Winton Road S., 14610
716-461-1620

Syracuse Syracuse Memorial Society, P.O. Box 67, De Witt, NY 13214-0067   315-446-0557

Yorktown Heights Funeral Cons. Info. Soc. of Westchester, 460 York Ct., 10598-3726   914-285-0585

North Carolina

Asheville Blue Ridge Memorial Society, P.O. Box 2601, 28802
828-669-2587

Charlotte Fun'l Consumers All'nce Centr'l Carolinas P.O. Box 26507, 28221   704-596-1208

Raleigh Fun'l Consumers All'nc/ Triangle, 1507 Doughton St., 27608-2521
919-834-6898

Wilmington Mem. Soc. of Coastal Carolina, P.O. Box 4262, 28406-4262

See South Dakota   *North Dakota*

Ohio

Akron Mem Soc of Akron-Canton Area, 3300 Morewood Road, 44333
330-849-1030 330-836-4418

Cincinnati Memorial Soc. of Greater Cincinnati, 536 Linton St., 45219

Cleveland Cleveland Memorial Society, 21600 Shaker Blvd., Shaker Heights, 44122   216-751-5515

Columbus Mem Soc of Columbus Area, P.O. Box 14835, 43214-4835
614-263-4632

Toledo Memorial Soc of Northwest Ohio, 2210 Collingwood Blvd., 43620-1147   419-475-1429

Oklahoma

All Oklahoma cities call 1-800-371-2221

Oregon

Portland Oregon Memorial Association, P.O. Box 25578, 97298
503-297-3513, (OR) 888-475-5520

Pennsylvania

Erie Memorial Society of Erie, Box 3495, 16508-3495   814-4564433

Harrisburg Mem. Soc. of Grtr Harrisburg, 1280 Clover Lane, 17113
717-564-8507

Philadelphia Mem. Soc. Grtr Philadelphia, 2125 Chestnut St., 19103
215-567-1065

Pittsburgh Pittsburgh Memorial Society, 605 Morewood Ave., 15213
412-621-4740

State College Mem. Soc. of Central PA, 780 Waupelani Dr. Ext., 16801
814-237-7605

Rhode Island

East Greenwich Mem. Soc. of R.I., 119 Kenyon Ave., 02818   401-884-1227

South Carolina

Columbia Funeral & Memorial Soc. of SC, 2701 Heyward St.,29205
803-772-7054

South Dakota

Lemmon Funeral Consumer Info. Soc. of Dakotas, 19168 Flat Creek Rd., - 57638   605-374-5336

Tennessee

Chattanooga Mem. Soc. of Chattanooga, 3224 Navajo Dr., 37411
423-886-3480
Knoxville East Tennessee Mem. Soc., P.O. Box 10507, 37939865-483-4843
Memphis Funeral Cons. All'nce of Mid South, P.O. Box 770388, 38177
901-685-2464, 901-680-9149
Nashville Middle Tennessee Mem. Soc., 1808 Woodmont Blvd., 37215
615-907-3364, 888-254-3872

Texas

Amarillo, El Paso, Lubbock, Rio Grand Valley Memorial Society of the Southwest, 2875 E. Parker Rd., Plano, 75074 800-371-2221 (TX/OK)
Austin Austin Mem. & Burial Info. Soc., P.O. Box 4382, 78765-4382
512-480-0555
Commerce, Dallas, Denton, Fort Worth, Longview, Tyler Memorial Society of North Texas 2875 E. Parker Rd., Plano, 75074
972-509-5686, 800-371-2221
Corpus Christi Mem. Soc of So. Texas 3125 Horne Rd., 78415
1-800-371-2221
Houston Funeral Consumers Alliance, Houston 5200 Fannin St., 77004-5899
713-526-4267, 888-282-4267
San Antonio San Antonio Memorial Society, 7150 Interstate 10 West, 78213   210-341-2213
Waco Mem. Soc. of N. Texas, Central TX Chapter 4209 N. 27th St., 76708-1509   800-371-2221

Utah

Orem Funeral Consumers Alliance of Utah, 1823 S 250 E, 84058-7840
801-226-4701

Vermont

East Montpelier Vermont Memorial Society & Cons. Alliance, 1630 Clark Rd., 05651
802-476-4300, 800-805-0007

Virginia

Arlington Memorial Society of No. Virginia, 4444 Arlington Blvd., 22204
703-271-9240
Charlottesville Mem. Planning Soc. of Piedmont, 717 Rugby Road, 22903
804-293-8179
Virginia Beach Memorial Soc. of Tidewater, P.O. Box 4621, 23454-4621
757-428-5134

Washington

Seattle People's Memorial Association, 2366 Eastlake Ave. E., Areis Bldg. #409, 98102   206-325-0489
Spokane Spokane Memorial Association, P.O. Box 13613, 99213-3613
509-924-8400
Yakima Funeral Assoc. Centrl Washington, P.O. Box 379, 98907
509-248-4533

West Virginia

Lewisburg Memorial Society of Greenbrier Valley, P.O. Box 1277, 24901

Morgantown & NE area: call MD Society
800-564-0017

Wisconsin

Egg Harbor Mem. Soc. of Wisconsin, 6900 Lost Lake Rd., 54209-9231
920-868-3136, (WI) 800-374-1109
Milwaukee Funeral Consumer Info. Soc. 13001 W. North Ave., Brookfield, 53005   262-238-0507

Call the FCA office   ***Wyoming***

Editor's Note: Most religious traditions include services for a time of death. The ceremonies in this appendix supplement these traditional services.

Memorial Services

On the following pages are several memorial services, each of which has been selected for some feature that seemed especially interesting. They have been compiled by Ann Baty of the Bowling Green, Ohio Memorial Society. Each of the first seven was written for a particular person who had died. Of the others, one is a general type of service that can be used for anyone. It is followed by two committal services—one for burial and one for cremation. The children's "good bye service" is not intended for a formal service but is meant to be used to help a child or children to cope with a grievous loss.

I. Service with Flower Communion

The memorial service for Esme Harold Naaman was prepared by a friend. Esme's death had ended several months of loving care given by friends who made it possible for him to die at home.

An order of service was mimeographed and folded into a booklet of ten pages plus cover. It contained the full text of all the selections that were used. It was mailed to friends and family who could not attend and served, for some, as a notice of Esme's death. The cover had his name and the dates of his birth and death with a paragraph about the kind of person he was.

After an interval of music by Bach and Brahms, as people gathered, the service began with these words: "We are a group of friends gathered together to pay loving tribute to Esme Naaman and to share with his family and each other our appreciation of a rare and remarkable human being."

Words written about him by a friend or two were read, as were a couple of letters that he had received (from brother and son) and that contained revealing sentiments. There were other readings: from *Voice of the Desert* by Joseph Wood Krutch, from *The Prophet* by Kahlil Gibran, and from Kenneth L. Patton. There were intervals of music (Sibelius, Croft, Mozart, Bach) and a short eulogy. A statement of the kind of person Esme had been was read by the minister.

Finally a friend said, "We invite you to take a blossom in our diverse remembrances of Esme." To the accompaniment of Bach's "Vater Unser in Himmelriech," four friends passed shallow baskets of chrysanthemum blossoms in yellow, bronze, and white as a flower communion; after that was a recitation of the Lord's Prayer and then a recessional by Bach.

The service was held in a Unitarian church, but was conducted by lay friends rather than by the minister.

II. Service Using Writings of the Deceased

Marcos Romero was a very creative young man from South America. While attending college in the United States, he was killed in a motorcycle accident. His friends put together this memorial service, using Marcos' own writings. The short service was held in a room in one of the college halls, and it was conducted entirely by students, his friends.

A program was printed and titled "Remembering Marcos Romero, A Service of Readings and Reflections." Date and place of the service also were printed on the cover.

The service began with a reading by a friend, followed by this litany:

LOVE ONE ANOTHER
Support one another's efforts
LOVE ONE ANOTHER
Rejoice in another's fulfillment
LOVE ONE ANOTHER
Support each other through difficult times
LOVE ONE ANOTHER
Rejoice together in times of rejoicing
LOVE ONE ANOTHER

Friends read from Marcos' writings, then sang a song written for Marcos by a friend. "Morning Has Broken" was sung by the group (the words were printed on the program).

There was a benediction from Marcos' writings: "Life is a matter of doing whatever has to be done with as much love as possible. By love, I mean concentration and dedication of one's life. I find that it is not so important to plan for the future, but to love everything we do and to let go and flow as a river flows."

The service ended with the reading of a poem written by Marcos Romero, titled "Good-bye: Dedicated to All Those Friends of Mine Who Listen."

III. Service with Organ Music

This service was arranged by friends of the deceased and was conducted by them. Harold Thomas Marlow had cared for his mother for many years until she died; he never married. After his mother died, he spent his time and energy working for his church; he left everything he had to the church.

The church had an organ and an organist, and most of the music was played by the organist. The service:

Prelude   Trumpet Tune in C and Trumpet Tune in D
—Purcell

Opening Words "Reasons for a Funeral or Memorial Service"
—Rev. Roy Phillips

We do best in our present and later lives if, when one we love dies, we bring together those whose lives were touched significantly by the one who has died. This is the reason for a funeral or a memorial service.

While such services have been understood in many varying ways, their human function is to set an experiential marker at the endpoint of life, to place a cairn at the conclusion of one human being's journey.

The cairns along a wilderness trail are built of earth rocks of various shapes and sizes. The memorial cairn at the end of a life is also a composite, but an experiential one. It is made up of the memories, the thoughts, and the feelings of all who are gathered in the one place together. It is a recollection (a re-collection) of what was for a time together and is now scattered and scattering. Here is the one we knew. This is how our lives were touched by that life. Here is what we think and how we feel.

The words spoken in the literal funeral or memorial service are not themselves the marker. The spoken words are evokers of experiences— thoughts, feelings, memories—within the people of the gathered group. These experiences are the memorial cairn.

At the end of a life, we compose a symphony, an ordered creation whose notes and themes are the experiences of the people gathered. Themes dark and bright are sounded to recollect and to order the impact of the life of the one who had died—honestly, fully, tenderly—and in the spirit of thanksgiving for the quality of that life.

The words of a memorial service should strive to evoke remembrance, thanksgiving, a sense of the uniqueness of the person's life, a sense of the privilege of having known that person, a sense of loss, of sadness, a feeling of emptiness, of unsureness, and a hint that the ending of this life is a rehearsal of what is to come for every one of us. The words should evoke a sense of trust in the slow but steady grace of healing and in the affirmation that we can live on and will live on, blessed by that life and by the memory of the one who once was and is now gone, but who is and will be present in the world, and in us, in mysterious and hidden ways.

Harold Thomas Marlow, scholar, churchman, friend, has died. We are gathered here to pay honor to his spirit and to the life he lived, and to consecrate his memory. The readings and music speak of him; reflect his spirit in life; reflect our feeling for him, and our feeling at this time.

Introit   "Well-Tempered Clavichord"
                                    —Bach

Readings "A Celebration for George Sarton" (final stanza)
                                    —May Sarton
              "On Death"
                                    —Kahlil Gibran

Solo   "Jesu, Joy of Man's Desiring"
                                    —Bach

Invitation to Thought

Words about Tom were spoken by the minister, and ending with this short meditation:

> Do you seek Tom Marlow? Why seek ye the living among the dead? All tombs are empty, signposts toward the silent mystery that is our origin and destiny. Seek the living among the living. Seek Tom in yourselves, in the patterns of your mind and memory, in the shape of the world made a little different by him, in the very rhythm of your heart of hearts. Amen.

Solo   "Pathetique Sonata, Andante Cantabile"
                                    —Beethoven

Eulogy   (read by a boyhood friend)

Solo   "Für Elise"
                                    —Beethoven

Reading   "There Are Men Too Gentle to Live Among Wolves*
                                    —James Kavanaugh

Music   "Suite in C"
                                    —Bach

Closing Words

> We, the living, have come together to ponder the death of one known to us, loved by us. We have come with sorrow that a good life should have to end. We have come with deep memories of our times with him, of joy and sorrow we shared with him, of the delightful and even the impatient moments we knew when he was with us. Here was a man, a man with hopes and dreams; a man with secret fears and unanswered questions; but a man with a zest for life and the strength to weather the storms that each of us must face. We, the living, give thanks that we have known Tom. We give thanks that he walked among us. We give thanks that he lived. Amen.

Postlude   "St. Anthony Chorale"
                                    —Haydn-Brahms

Sources

The readings suggested in this service can be found in the following sources: May Sarton, *Collected Poems: 1930–1973,* Norton, 1974; Kahlil Gibran, *The Prophet*, Alfred A. Knopf; James Kavanaugh, *There Are Men Too Gentle to Live Among Wolves*, Dutton, 1970.

Our apologies to the four-legged wolves. They are not the ones referred to in this poem. As Farley Mowatt says, "Never Cry Wolf" unless you specify which kind.

IV. Service Held for a Teenage Girl

Mary, sixteen, was killed while on vacation with her family. Her body was cremated with a private committal service.

When the family returned to their home, a memorial service was held in the United Methodist church to which they belonged. Significant objects relating to Mary, things she prized, graced the chancel area.

Music significant to the family, including "Bridge Over Troubled Water," was played.

The pastor spoke sentences of hope and comfort from the Scriptures, and he read the Twenty-third Psalm. He prayed, and the congregation prayed the Lord's Prayer in unison. They sang "Precious Lord."

The youth minister read portions of the eighth chapter of Romans and preached on the text, ". . . the Spirit himself intercedes for us with sighs too deep for words." (Rom. 8:26 RSV)

A friend sang "One Day at a Time."

Those present were invited to share their thoughts about Mary with one another as the spirit moved them. (Mary's high school English teacher read from Mary's writings. One of her brothers read a poem she had written. Her father and mother, referring to the objects in the room and recent conversations with Mary, expressed their grief and hope and their need for the community of love.)

The congregation sang "Joy Is Like the Rain."

They were invited to come forward and stand with family for Holy Communion. The minister took the bread and a cup, gave thanks, broke the bread—a loaf baked by a friend—and gave the bread and the cup to the people, who served one another hand to hand.

They sang "Amazing Grace," received the benediction, and sang "Shalom"—the congregation's customary closing song. The people spontaneously shared their love with the family, and then gradually dispersed.

—from *Abingdon Funeral Manual* by Perry H. Biddle, Jr.
Quoted with permission, Abingdon Press, Nashville Tenn.

V. a Memorial Walk

A "Memorial Walk" was held for Steve Persons on a Sunday afternoon at the small golf course in the mobile home park where he had been living. Steve had been an avid golfer for many years and many friends knew him best in the golf setting.

Steve's friends gathered at the designated entrance to a path that followed the edge of the greens toward the mobile home park clubhouse just two short blocks away. The family arrived and led the group along the path to a midpoint bordering the golf course, where a large oak tree spread its branches. Here they stopped. Some sat on a bench beneath the tree as the friends grouped themselves around the family. While those in attendance absorbed the beauty of the golf course where Steve had spent so many happy hours, his nephew spoke some words of greeting, then gave a biographical sketch of Steve's life. Two of Steve's favorite songs were played on a cassette tape recorder, after which a friend spoke briefly and respectfully about Steve's interests and accomplishments in the world of music. The family then led the walk to the clubhouse entrance, where they turned and greeted their friends who passed through the door into the building.

Inside, the group found seats in the informal lounge. Simple refreshments were served while favorite classical piano selections were played. People were able to relax comfortably to talk to each other and the family, and especially to talk with relatives from afar whom they had not seen for a long time.

This memorial service, though quite simple, was very comforting and filled with love. Real support and sympathy was shown to the family as they and their friends exchanged incidents, anecdotes, and many remembrances about their beloved Steve throughout the rest of the afternoon.

VI. An Unstructured Service Held in a Farmyard

This was a service held for Tom Blank. He had grown up on a farm near a small city. He had lived in the same community all of his life. After he died, his brother arranged for a memorial service held outdoors in the farmyard, just as Tom once, years before, had said he'd like it to be.

Chairs were carried out onto the lawn; a table of soft drinks was set up at one side. A rowboat that Tom had enjoyed using on the river in his playtime hours was filled with garden and field flowers; it also held a self-portrait Tom had painted.

There were some prepared readings, but guests were invited to, and did, speak as the spirit moved them to do so about their love for Tom.

VII. A Quaker Service

A man describes the unplanned service for his wife as "The most beautiful and meaningful memorial service I ever attended."

She had become a very active and devoted Friend (Quaker) after having been a Catholic for more than sixty years. She died very early on a Saturday morning. A friend of hers went all over the campus (where they taught) and spread the word to all her friends, asking them to attend the regular Sunday morning service of the Friends meeting—even if they were not Quakers. And they did. "In the traditional Quaker manner," the gentleman writes, "all sat around in a circle with only a rug and a large candle in the center, and a number of those who knew her spoke feelingly of what she had meant to them, and what she had done for other people. There were no rehearsed speeches, no eulogy by someone who had to be briefed. The testimonies were given from firsthand experience and from the heart . . . and at the end, all joined hands with their neighbors, in accordance with their custom."

VIII. Love Memorial for Our Son (as described by his mother)

Scott had been a skydiver for ten years, with over two thousand jumps and twenty-four hours of freefall. His skydiving had taken him all over the United States and Europe. He had always assured me, when I worried, that he was safer in the air than driving on the highway.

We were totally unprepared, therefore, for the news of his death a thousand miles away from home. We didn't know what to do. We were aware of the local memorial society; we weren't members, but we knew people who were. We called them and got the telephone number of the memorial society in Tampa, where Scott had been killed. We called there, and they put us in touch with a funeral home. Scott's body was cremated. Everyone was most helpful and thoughtful. The ashes were brought back with Scott's belongings and his car.

We wanted to have a very special and beautiful memorial service for our son; he was a very special and beautiful person. We also wanted his ten-year-old daughter to have something beautiful to remember. At first we weren't sure just how to go ahead; suddenly ideas began coming. I believe Scott must have been helping me; even the poem we used for a memorial card was the first one I looked at.

All our family and friends helped. There was no time to get printing done, nor to order special paper. Our daughter made up a sample memorial card, and we had quick-print copies made on stationery.

The urn, with ashes, was placed in a cut crystal bowl surrounded by red and white rose petals with a tall basket of red and white carnations on each side for the service in the Catholic church. From the church everyone went to the park on the river, where Scott had been best man at his brother's wedding some months before. A service was held there, while Scott's skydiving team flew over the river and scattered the ashes together with a bushel of rose petals. A red or white carnation was given to each of those gathered there to cast upon the water with their special love and a prayer for Scott. Sheri, Scott's daughter, cast a white rosebud.

Since there were a great many people from out of town, we asked everyone to come to our house for refreshments, which had been brought in and were served by our wonderful friends and neighbors. We all shared our memories of Scott; his skydiving awards were presented to us at that time.

IX. Recognition of Death

(Adapted from *The Book of Celebration* by Duke T. Gray and from "A Humanist Funeral Service" by Corliss Lamont and distributed by the Memorial Society of London, P.O. Box 1279, Station A, London, Ontario N6A 5H9.)

This service may be used either for a funeral service, with the body present, or for a memorial service following burial or cremation. Either service may be done in a church or elsewhere. It is designed to include congregational participation if copies can be made available so that those gathered can take part. This is an important way of helping to evoke the grief and hope that must have their expression. Otherwise, the minister or someone else may simply read the unison or responsive parts.

Music (optional)

Responsive Reading
Reader: Oh, Death, where is your sting?
           Oh, Grave, where is your victory?

Unison: Peace be with us.
Reader: We must all die, and are as water spilt on the ground,
              which cannot be gathered up again.
Unison: Peace be with us.
Reader: Set me as a seal upon your heart, as a seal upon your
              arm: for love is strong as death.
Unison: Peace be with us.
Reader: Blessed are those who mourn, for they shall be
              comforted.
Unison: Peace be with us.
Reader: Blessed are you who weep now, for you shall laugh.
Unison: Peace be with us.
Reader: I have set before you life and death, blessing and
              cursing: Therefore choose life, that both you and your
              descendants may live.
Unison: Peace be with us.
Reader: And now abide faith, hope and love, these three; but
              the greatest of these is love.

The Welcome

Let us call to memory the dead, yet ever living, who have passed the doors beyond which we cannot see. They dwell at peace in the halls of memory, whose hallowed treasure it is ours to keep from this day forward.

We have gathered in this place to do honor and praise to the life and memory of _____. We have gathered to offer thanksgiving and gratitude that one such as he/she has lived among us. We have gathered in celebration of death, and in so doing, in celebration of life—for life and death are one, even as the river flows to the sea.

(A candle may be lighted)

Opening Prayer (in unison)

Holy Spirit of Life, and of peace in death, lift our sorrows.
Beloved memory and fragile hope, heal the wounds of our mortal loss.
Indestructible remembrance, in whom the spirits of the departed do rest
    from their labors:
We bless you for the memory of those most dear to us, who have lived in
    joy and departed in peace.
May we follow the best in them, and truly loving and serving the gifts they
    gave us,
Be gathered with them into the life abundant, against whose very richness
The forces of death cannot prevail. Amen.

The Circle of Life

Reader: To everything there is a season
Unison: And a time to every purpose under heaven:

Reader:	A time to be born, and a time to die;
Unison:	A time to plant, and a time to harvest;
Reader:	A time to kill, a time to heal;
Unison:	A time to break, and a time to build;
Reader:	A time to weep, and a time to laugh;
Unison:	A time to mourn, and a time to dance
Reader:	A time to cast away stones, and a time to bring stones together;
Unison:	A time to embrace, and a time to be apart;
Reader:	A time to get, and a time to lose;
Unison:	A time to keep silence, a time to speak;
Reader:	We should rejoice in our works, for that is our portion;
Unison:	Cast your bread upon the waters; for you shall find it after many days.

—Ecclesiastes

Music (if desired)

Readings
(Readings, remarks, and a eulogy or biographical sketch)

"In Memory of W.B. Yeats" (final stanza)

—W.H. Auden

"On Death" from *The Prophet*

—Kahlil Gibran

Closing Prayer
Now the work is left to us, the living, to carry forth the beauty and joy of this life that has been taken from us. Where we weep, he/she would have us laugh. Where we mourn, he/she would have us rejoice. But we know that he/she will forgive us our grief, for to grieve is to love, to love is to cherish, and to cherish is to give praise and thanksgiving for the life that has blessed us all. To that life we pray courage and strength, that our frailty be forgiven, our sorrows redeemed, the wounds of our loss healed, in the sure knowledge that life moves forward and does not tarry with yesterday, and that the life before us beckons to greater glory as the only memorial that is fitting and just. Amen.

X. Committal Services

A Committal Service for Cremation: Most crematories have an adjacent chapel or an anteroom in which people may gather for a brief ceremony of committal just before the cremation process begins:

In committing the body of _____ to the flames, we do so with deep reverence for that body as the temple, during life, of a unique and beloved personality. Through the purifying process of fire, this body now becomes transformed into the more simple and ultimate elements of our universe. Fire is, itself, one of the great forces of nature.

"Fruit-Gathering" by Sir Rabindranath Tagore (See "Selected Readings," pages 139–140,144.)

To the flame, then, we give finally the body of our friend with the full and certain knowledge that, in the words of Socrates, "No evil can befall a good man either in life or after death."

Benediction
Let us depart in peace, and look to the morning, assured that tomorrow the sun will rise again.
Life gives, and life takes away; blessed be life, above all, forever. Amen.

Alternative Benediction
Now, for us, the living,
may the love of friends,
the radiance of memory,
the fellowship of hope,
and the life abundant
fill us with all strength and peace,
that we may greet the breaking
of tomorrow's dawn with praise. Amen.

An Interment Service for Burial: This is a service held at the grave site at the time of burial; sometimes it is called a graveside.

Opening Words
Whatsoever things are true,
Whatsoever things are honest,
Whatsoever things are just,
Whatsoever things are pure,
Whatsoever things are lovely,
Whatsoever things are of good report:
    if there be any virtue, and if there be any praise,
Think on these things.
                            —(based on *Phil. 4:8*)

We know in part, and we prophesy in part.
But when that which is perfect is come,
    that which is in part shall be done away.
For now we see through a glass darkly;
    but then face to face;
Now I know in part; but then shall I know

even as also I am known.

—(based on 1 Cor. 13)

Prayer

Reader: In the midst of life, we are in death.

   Let us know full well that the spirit of our beloved dwells
    now in our hearts;

   Let us seek the courage, in love, to carry forward
    his/her memory in the lives we now lead.

Unison: Holy Spirit of Life, receive from us the person of _____.

   Let the best which was in him/her, be renewed in
    strength in us.

   May we now give to others the love that we no longer
    can give to him/her,

   For the lives we lead are now his/her honor and memorial.

   He/she would bless our sorrows with courage.

   May our time of pain issue in larger peace.

   He/she would wish it so;

   So let it be. Amen.

Burial

For as much as the spirit of our brother/sister dwells no more in this mortal form, we commit the body to the ground—earth to earth, ashes to ashes, dust to dust—in the sure knowledge that his/her life continues in us, and that his/her works abide upon the earth. The torch he/she lit, we now carry forward, as also others will pass along ours.

   [A flower may be tossed into the grave.]

   Down gently, down.
   Softer to sleep
   than bed of night.
   From the littleness,
   Go.
   Down gently, down.
   Wider to wake
   Than need of sun.
   Into the greatness,
   Go.

XI. A Good-bye Ceremony for Children Who Grieve

This ceremony was developed in a workshop on celebrations. This workshop tried to create ceremonies for those special situations that are important in our lives but that are not customarily noted with a ceremony. One group chose to develop an observance to mark the death of a child's pet, but as they talked, they realized that there are other deaths that might affect a child very deeply—not the devastating loss of a parent or sibling; that would be a different problem altogether.

They were thinking of those incomprehensible, bewildering deaths, such as the death of a friend, of a good neighbor, of a slightly known or distant relative, of a teacher.

This ceremony is intended to help a child cope with grief and bewilderment and outrage. It can easily be held at home, but could be held in a schoolroom. It can be conducted by parents (or a parent) for a single child, or for several children. It is important that the expressions be honest—use words like death, sorrow, grief—not euphemisms. It's all right to cry. Begin with a statement of purpose, such as:

> We've gathered together today to remember with love our friend, Jill, who has died. All living things must die, as we, too, will someday die. It makes us sad that this is so, but no thing lives forever.
>   *[Read a poem, or have some music.]*

Light a candle and say something like:

> "We light this candle. The light will symbolize for us Jill's life, as we think of how much we loved her. Although our sadness is great, we also think how glad we are that she lived, and we are thankful that we knew her, for we had happy times together. If we had some bad times, too, they aren't important now. We loved her; she was a good friend, we'll miss her very much."
>   *[Music, or read a poem.]*

Candle Lighting Service: Provide several small candles, and arrange it so that each one can safely be left standing near the large candle—perhaps on a metal tray or in a tray of damp sand. Each child takes a candle, and lighting it at the large candle, says:

> I remember . . . [something to do with Jill]

then places the small burning candle near the large burning candle.

Extinguish the large candle, saying something like:

> Jill herself has died, but memories of her, symbolized by these smaller candles, keep on glowing in our hearts and minds, just as the candles keep on glowing.

  Do not extinguish the candles, let them burn down. Or, if the children are going to leave, let them leave while the candles are still burning.

If this is a ceremony for a pet, it could end with burial.
To use flowers instead of candles, have a large bouquet from which each child takes a flower as memories are recalled.

The children should understand, from what you say to them, that although the flowers will fade and die, because nothing living lasts forever, their memories will live on in their minds.

Selected Readings[1]

The following readings are offered for use in planning memorial, funeral, and committal services. They are intended to supplement biblical and other materials commonly available in reference works for clergy of various faiths.

Wise selection is the key to the effective use of readings. The sensibilities and wishes of the family should be the determining factor.

The readings offer perspective, too, to those contemplating their own death, or reflecting on past bereavement. They can be a source of inspiration and understanding for all students of death education.

General Readings

We meet here in the presence of death to do homage to the Spirit of Life. We would feign make this hour Love's hour and these simple rites Love's confessional. For it is Love's tribute that we come to offer here today.

Our voices may be the voices of grief, but the language after which grief gropes is the language of Love. And we who gather here come in Love's name to express, for those whose lives have been bereft of Love's visible presence, a calm and abiding trust in Love's immortality and consecrating power.

—Robert Terry Weston

No one entering this world can ever escape sadness. Each in his turn must bear his burdens, though he be rich or poor, and in his turn bid his loved ones farewell as they set out upon life's ventures. Each one must suffer that sad farewell when loved ones embark on the last voyage, and each in turn must himself take that final journey into the dark.

But to those who make this life a pledge to light and spirit there comes the assurance of a victory that shall redeem life's pain. Though our spirit be but the feeble glow of a candle, there is no dark that it cannot pierce. For him who keeps the candle burning bravely to the end, death is not defeat for light goes on.

—Robert Terry Weston

Bitter is the sorrow of bereavement, yet when a loved one passes, remember then the blessing we have received: rejoice that even for so brief a period our life has been enriched and deepened beyond the power of anything to destroy, for never beauty touched the heart of man without creating something eternal.

—Robert Terry Weston

And yet I say unto you, be of good courage, for although you may not escape sadness, it is because the life that has departed was rich and sweet that you are sad, and whatever has worth and dignity and beauty is not lost.

Nay, this is the testimony not only of the ages since the dawn of time, but this is the message of the test tube and the telescope, even as prophets have proclaimed and poets sung, that nothing is ever lost, but that all things change and move throughout eternity. And dare we not believe that life itself shall be conserved, though bodies die and pass into the earth: yea, and that spirit through the crucible of mortality is not destroyed but purified and enriched and made more great?

—Robert Terry Weston

Gitanjali—87

In desperate hope I go and search for her in all the corners of my room; I find her not.

My house is small and what once has gone from it can never be regained.

But infinite is thy mansion, my lord, and seeking her I have come to thy door.

I stand under the golden canopy of thine evening sky and I lift my eager eyes to thy face.

I have come to the brink of eternity from which nothing can vanish—no hope, no happiness, no vision of a face seen through tears.

Oh, dip my emptied life into that ocean, plunge it into the deepest fullness. Let me for once feel that lost sweet touch in the allness of the universe.

—Rabindranath Tagore

Gitanjali—84

It is the pang of separation that spreads throughout the world and gives birth to shapes innumerable in the infinite sky.

It is this sorrow of separation that gazes in silence all night from star to star and becomes lyric among rustling leaves in rainy darkness of July.

It is this overspreading pain that deepens into loves and desires, into sufferings and joys in human homes; and this it is that ever melts and flows in songs through my poet's heart.

—Rabindranath Tagore

Gitanjali—90

"On the day when death shall knock at thy door, what wilt thou offer him?

"Oh, I will set before my guest the full vessel of my life—I will never let him go with empty hands.

"All the sweet vintage of my autumn days and summer nights, all the earnings and gleanings of my busy life will I place before him at the close of my days when death will knock at my door."

When I finished she remarked that her vessel was full.

—Rabindranath Tagore

Crossing the Bar

Sunset and evening star,
And one clear call for me!

And may there be no moaning of the bar,
    When I put out to sea,
But such a tide as moving seems asleep,
    Too full for sound and foam,
When that which drew from out the boundless deep
    Turns again home.
Twilight and evening bell,
    And after that the dark!
And may there be no sadness of farewell,
    When I embark;
For though from out our bourne of Time and Place
    The flood may bear me far,
I hope to see my Pilot face to face
    When I have crossed the bar.

—Alfred, Lord Tennyson

Fruit-Gathering: XLVI

The time is past when I could repay her for all that I received.
Her night has found its morning and thou hast taken her to thy arms: and
    to thee I bring my gratitude and my gifts that were for her.
For all hurts and offenses to her I come to thee for forgiveness.
I offer to thy service those flowers of my love that remained in bud when
    she waited for them to open.

—Rabindranath Tagore

Fruit-Gathering: XLIX

The pain was great when the strings were being tuned, my Master!
Begin your music, and let me forget the pain; let me feel in beauty what
    you had in your mind through those pitiless days.
The waning night lingers at my doors, let her take her leave in songs.
Pour your heart into my life strings, my Master, in tunes that descend from
    your stars.

—Rabindranath Tagore

In Memoriam: LIII

O yet we trust that somehow good
    Will be the final goal of ill,
    To pangs of nature, sins of will,
Defects of doubt, and taints of blood;
That nothing walks with aimless feet;
    That not one life shall be destroy'd,
    Or cast as rubbish to the void,
When God hath made the pile complete;
That not a worm is cloven in vain;
    That not a moth with vain desire
    Is shrivel'd in a fruitless fire,

Or but subserves another's gain.
Behold, we know not anything;
   I can but trust that good shall fall
   At last—far off—at last, to all.
And every winter change to spring.
So runs my dream: but what am I?
   An infant crying in the night:
   An infant crying for the light:
And with no language but a cry.

—Alfred, Lord Tennyson

O God, eternal spirit of love and righteousness, through whose constant presence in our hearts we are made strong, and by whom we live, we come unto thee in this time of sorrow, and we are sustained by thine indwelling presence.

Thou teachest us to be reconciled unto sorrow; thou turnest sorrow into a universal sympathy and compassion. Trusting in thee we learn not merely to endure but to rejoice in life as a far more eternal and abiding thing than human flesh.

Not for ourselves along, but for all who suffer and are afflicted by grief, we pray, that consciousness of thine eternity of fulfillment may uplift and sustain, and thy compassion minister to them through human hands.

May we learn to be glad for that which has been, not as something taken away but as something given to us even if for a brief time, through which we have been blessed. Teach us, we pray, to rejoice again, to share all beauty we have known, all love, all hope, all faith, and to be grateful for they tender hand which at the end bringeth release in peace and blessed sleep.

—Robert Terry Weston

I had rather think of those I have loved and lost as having returned to earth, as having become a part of the elemental wealth of the world, I would rather dream of them as unconscious dust; I would rather dream of them as laughing in the stream, floating in the clouds, bursting in light upon the shores of other worlds; I would rather think of them as the lost visions of a forgotten night, than to have even the faintest fear . . . But as for me, I will leave the dead where nature leaves them. Whatever flower of hope springs in my heart I will cherish; I will give it breath of sighs and rain of tears.

—R.G. Ingersoll, "The House of Death"

O thou, who art the inspirer of the faith that burns ever more brightly within the souls of men, unto thee do we turn in this time of testing. Within us do well up the great mysteries of the ages. The unanswered questions of all saddened hearts are on our lips. We would be assured and comforted if that might be within the power of our hearts to know and understand. But as we pause to honor a memory made beautiful by life, we pray only that our faith be strengthened by the faith that was so strong in him.

Maker of Mysteries, guide thou us whose spiritual vision is dim and uncertain. As the joy of close comradeship is withdrawn, do thou come with thy divine fellowship and renew our confidence in the everlasting life of the spirit of man.

—Francis G. Ricker

Mourn Not the Dead

Mourn not the dead that in the cool earth lie
Dust unto dust—
The calm, sweet earth that mothers all who die
As all men must;

But rather mourn the apathetic throng—
The cowed and meek
Who see the world's great anguish and its wrong
And dare not speak!

—Ralph Chaplin

A Scriptural Message for Use in a Memorial Service
by *Rev. Philip Nordstrom* (adapted):

God is our refuge and strength, our constant help in every sorrow;
Therefore we will not fear even though this earthly dust be removed and be carried into the Eternal Sea,
For therein is a river whose fountains gladden the City of God, the holy temples of his dwelling place.
Come behold now this work of the Lord, what transformations he hath wrought on this earth, in this holy clay:
He hath made an end to this transitory struggle,
He hath unbent this bow, and shattered the shaft,
And he hath refined as in fire, this mortal chariot unto immortality.

[Based on *Psalm 46*]

Comfort ye, comfort ye, my people, saith your God.
Speak ye comfortably to Jerusalem and say unto her that her iniquity is pardoned.
For he shall lead his flock like a shepherd,
He shall carry the lambs in his arms and gently lead those that are with young.
Have you not known?
Have you not heard that the everlasting God, the creator of the ends of the earth fainteth not, neither is weary.
For he giveth power to the faint and to them that have no might
He increaseth strength.

They shall walk and not faint, they shall run and not be weary, they shall mount up with wings as eagles.   [*Isaiah 40:1–2, 11, 28–31*]

Behold, I will not leave you comfortless, but I will come unto you, and I will make my abode with you, and will come in and sup with you.
[*John 14*]

In this world, ye shall have tribulation but be of good cheer, I have overcome the world.   [*John 16:33*]

My peace I give unto you; not as the world gives, give I unto you.
[*John 14:27*]

Behold! I will give you the oil of gladness instead of mourning, and sorrowing and sighing shall be done away.   [*Isaiah 61:3*]

Come unto Me, all ye that labor and are heavy laden and I will give you rest.
Take my yoke upon you and learn of me, for I am meek and lowly in heart, for my yoke is easy and my burden is light.
[*Matthew 11:28–30*]

Incline your ear, and come unto me, hear, and your soul shall live.
[*Isaiah 56:3*]

Remember that the eternal God is thy refuge and underneath are the everlasting arms.
Comfort ye! Comfort ye, my people!
Says your God.

Readings for a Child

We are hurting, Lord. With our child's death went all our hopes, our dreams, our future.

But in our grief we can now fully appreciate the little things in life. We are thankful for even the short time we had with our child. We realize how fragile and brief life can be. We now take nothing for granted.

Thank you for being with us in our time of sadness and grief. We look to you for strength.

—From burial service for Benjamin Matthew Jones

In the flesh there is no continuing life, for things that are of flesh must perish after the way of flesh; yet there is no spirit however weak or faint, however young, but leaves its glow upon the world; no spirit, however long or short its sojourn here, but speaks of greater and enduring life through its own sublime mystery and beauty. The spirit is of the nature of eternity:

even as it smiles upon us here, suddenly there is a light about our heads and life is changed. So this bright spark of the eternal fire is not lost in death. The first brave smile of the tiniest babe kindles a warmth in other hearts that shall never die. Though death strike sorrow to our hearts, the glory of that smile still lingers within, to outlive sorrow and bind us to all childhood with enfolding love.   —*Robert Terry Weston*

Readings for the Aged

Beautiful are the youth whose rich emotions flash and burn, whose lithe bodies filled with energy and grace sway in their happy dance of life; and beautiful likewise are the mature who have learned compassion and patience, charity and wisdom, though they be rarer far than beautiful youth. But most beautiful and most rare is a gracious old age which has drawn from life the skill to take its varied strands: the harsh advance of age, the pang of grief, the passing of dear friends, the loss of strength, and with fresh insight weave them into a rich and gracious pattern all its own. This is the greatest skill of all, to take the bitter with the sweet and make it beautiful, to take the whole of life in all its moods, its strengths and weaknesses, and of the whole make one great and celestial harmony.
                                                      —*Robert Terry Weston*

Readings for a Parent

Blessed are they who rear their families in honor and in gentleness, who live courageous and upright lives, who live life in its fullness, do their part, and then at eventide retire to rest.

Though pain be in the heart, let none grieve, for here a gentle soul has cast its glow upon us, and like the glory of an autumn sun, has lit the world with kindness through its day, and at the close has gently sunk to rest.

Rather rejoice for that which (she) has given, the light we know and treasure still within our hearts, a light we trust still shineth beyond the distant peaks (this world's horizon), for life goes on, and spirit knows no death.   —*Robert Terry Weston*

Readings for Burial Committal Services

Requiem

Fall softly, O thou coat of winter snow, and keep our loved one warm;
Kiss him gently, sun and rain, in the quiet of his rest;
Watch over him, wind and stars, in the silence of the night;
Grow thou to cover him, grass and flowers, and make beautiful his couch,
And thou, Great Spirit of Love and Peace, take him into thine arms and lull
     him to rest forevermore. Amen.
                                                    —*Rev. John G. MacKinnon*

Deep wet moss and cool blue shadows
    Beneath a bending fir,
And the purple solitude of mountains,
    When only the dark owls stir—
Oh, there will come a day, a twilight,
    When I shall sink to rest
In deep wet moss and cool blue shadows
    Upon a mountain's breast,
And yield a body torn with passions,
    And bruised with earthly scars,
To the cool oblivion of evening,
    Of solitude and stars.

—Lew Sarett

Song

She's somewhere in the sunlight strong,
Her tears are in the falling rain,
She calls me in the wind's soft song.
And with the flowers she comes again.
Yon bird is but her messenger,
The moon is but her silver car;
Yea! sun and moon are sent by her,
And every wistful waiting star.

—Richard LeGallienne

Readings for Cremation Committal Service

Fruit-Gathering:XL

O Fire, my brother, I sing victory to you.
You are the bright red image of fearful freedom.
You swing your arms in the sky, you sweep your impetuous fingers across
    the harp-string, your dance music is beautiful.
When my days are ended and the gates are opened you will burn to ashes
    this cordage of hands and feet.
My body will be one with you, my heart will be caught in the whirls of
    your frenzy, and the burning heat that was my
life will flash up and mingle itself in your flame.

—Rabindranath Tagore

It is but fitting that we should commit this body to the flame
So like that which but recently did burn
Within that fine brave head.
It is as if he doth return
Unto the fountain whence he came,
Source of all spirits bright,
The comradeship and life of all pure souls,

As now he enters into purifying light.

—Robert Terry Weston

Additional Readings
"To W.P. II." by George Santayana
"Dirge Without Music," by Edna St. Vincent Millay
"Death," "Joy and Sorrow," and "Pain," from *The Prophet* by Kahlil Gibran.
Psalms 19, 23, and 121.

ENDNOTE

[1]Quotations by Robert Terry Weston, R.G. Ingersoll, Francis G. Ricker, Rev. John G. MacKinnon, and Richard LeGallienne, are taken from *A Cup of Strength: Readings in Time of Sorrow and Bereavement*, compiled by Robert Terry Weston, 1945. Reprinted by permission from Robert Terry Weston.

INFORMATION AND COORDINATION

The American Association of Tissue Banks. 1350 Beverly Rd., Suite 220-A, McLean, VA 22101; 703-827-9582; fax 703-356-2198. Nongovernmental group of physicians, nurses, lawyers, technicians, and the general public. Develops standards for tissue banking. Inspects and certifies tissue banks. Certifies personnel. Persons requesting tissue may call 800-635-2282.

Eye Bank Association of America. 1001 Connecticut Ave. NW, Washington DC 20036-5504; 202-775-4999. Develops standards, professional training, and computer coordination; monitors government activity and the media.

Eye Bank of Canada (Ontario Division). c/o The Canadian Institute for the Blind, 1929 Bayview Avenue, Toronto, Ontario M4G 3E8. Clearinghouse for Canadian eye banks.

The Living Bank. P.O. Box 6725, Houston, TX 77265; 800-528-2971 (URL: *http://www.livingbank.org*). A central registry for persons wishing to donate organs or tissues at time of death. Send for a registration form. See Chapter 8.

Medic Alert. Turlock, CA 95381-1009; 209-668-3333. See Chapter 8, "How the Dead Can Help the Living."

Organ Donors Canada. 5326 Ada Boulevard, Edmonton, Alberta T5W 4N7; 403-474-9363. Founded in 1974, this is a nonprofit lay organization devoted to increasing public awareness of the need for organ and tissue donation.

Transplant International. 339 Windermere Rd., London, Ont. N6A 5A5; 519-663-3709. Publishes free quarterly newsletter called "Transplant Lifelines."

United Network for Organ Sharing (UNOS). P.O. Box 13770, Richmond, VA 23225; 804-330-8500. Founded in 1977, a nationwide computerized network for matching transplant donations and recipients through its membership of 275 transplant centers, 63 independent organ procurement agencies, and 50 tissue typing laboratories. Since 1986 UNOS has had a federal contract to operate the National Procurement and Transplantation Network (OPTN) and the National Scientific Registry.

Uniform Donor Cards

Uniform donor cards may be obtained from American Association of Tissue Banks, The Living Bank, Medic Alert, and Organ Donors Canada, addresses above; and from the Funeral and Memorial Societies of America (FAMSA), see Appendix 6, "Directory of Funeral Consumer Information Societies," and Kidney Foundations, addresses in this appendix.

Canadian Regional Organ Procurement and Exchange Programs

ALBERTA: Human Organ Procurement and Exchange Program, Foothills Provincial General Hospital, 1403 29th St. NW, Calgary, AB T2N 2T9. 403-283-2243.
Human Organ Procurement and Exchange Program, University of Alberta Hospitals, 8440 112 St., Edmonton, AB T6G 2B7. 403-492-1970.

BRITISH COLUMBIA: Pacific Organ Retrieval for Transplantation, Vancouver General Hospital, 855 12th Avenue, Vancouver, BC V5Z 1M9. 604-875-4665.

MANITOBA: Manitoba Transplant Program, Health Sciences Centre, 700 William Avenue, Winnipeg, MB R3E 0Z3. 204-787-2071 Ext. 505.

NEW BRUNSWICK: Organ Procurement for Transplantation, St. John Regional Hospital, Saint John, NB E2L 4L2. 506-648-6848.

NEWFOUNDLAND: Organ Procurement and Exchange Program, Health Sciences Complex, St. John's, NF A1B 3V6. 709-737-6600.

NOVA SCOTIA: Multi-Organ Transplant Program, Victoria General Hospital, Halifax, NS B3H 2Y9. 902-428-5504.

ONTARIO: Multiple Organ Retrieval and Exchange Program, 200 Elizabeth St., Toronto, ON M5C 2G4. 800-387-MORE / 416-595-3587.

QUEBEC: Metro Transplantaion, 1560 Sherbrooke St. E., Montreal, QC H2L 4KB. 514-876-6768.

SASKATCHEWAN: Renal Transplant Program, University Hospital, Saskatoon, SK S7N 0X0. 306-966-7985.

Related Legislation

The National Organ Transplant Act was passed by the United States Congress in 1984. It provided for a task force to study the "medical, legal, ethical, economic, and social issues presented by human organ procurement and transplantation." The act authorizes the funding of the contracted Organ Procurement and Transplantation Network as a clearinghouse for transplant centers, and prohibits the purchase of organs.

In 1982, the U.S. Conference of Commissioners on Uniform State Laws recommended a Uniform Determination of Death Act and most states now have effected this act or an equivalent. This defines death as the irreversible cessation of all brain and brain stem function, thus allowing artificial maintenance of heartbeat and respiration to preserve needed organs without raising doubt that the person is in fact dead.

In Canada, all provinces have now adopted some form of the Model Human Tissues Gift Act recommended by the Conference of Commissioners on Uniformity of Legislation in Canada in 1970.

SPECIFIC ANATOMICAL GIFTS[1]

Eyes. The most frequently transplanted of all human tissues (except blood and bone tissues) are the corneas, or lenses of the eyes. Thousands of blind people have had their sight restored in this way. In 1998 there were 2,515 corneas transplanted in Canada. In the United States in 1999, 50,789 corneas were used for transplant and other surgical procedures. Not all vision defects can be cured by transplants, and it is not possible to transplant the whole eye, but sight can be restored in most cases of common corneal diseases. In North America there are thousands of blind people whose sight could be restored if enough corneas were available. In 1997 35,047 corneas were used for training and research.

Always carry a Uniform Donor Card and be sure to check the Eye Bank square. Call your nearest eye bank for instructions on how to assure that your gift is used, and for more information on how eye donations are used in your area. It does not matter if you wear glasses or what your age, race, or blood type may be. Eyes must be removed by trained personnel within a few hours of death. This can be done in the hospital or at home. Some funeral directors are trained to do this. Eyes may not be bequeathed to specific individuals, but must be used on a first-come first-served basis regardless of ability to pay. Airlines transport them without charge. Unlike other organs, the donation of eyes does not prevent leaving one's body to a medical school. Likewise, it makes no difference in the appearance of the body for viewing.

To Locate an Eye Bank: There are 108 eye banks in the United States and Canada that are members of the Eye Bank Association, and additional ones are being added from time to time.

To locate an eye bank in Canada write or call Eye Bank of Canada (Ontario Division), 1 Spadina Crescent, Toronto, ON M5S 2J5; 416-978-2637 / 486-2520. To locate one in the United States, write or call the Eye Bank Association, 1001 Connecticut Ave., NW, Washington, DC 20036-5504; 202-775-4999.

Kidneys. First and most frequent of major organs to be transplanted, 112,483 kidneys were transplanted in the U.S. in 1999. (Of these, 4,698 were from living donors.) In another 946 cases, kidneys plus pancreases were transplanted.. Patient survival rates after one year are now as high as ninety-seven percent for kidneys from related donors, and ninety percent with cadaver organs. Back in 1985 in the United States nearly 85,000 patients were kept alive by artificial kidney machines (dialysis), of whom 10,000 were waiting for a kidney transplant. By June, 2000, 45,521 patients were waiting for kidney transplants in the United States, plus 2,328 more waiting for kidney-pancreas transplants. Thousands more donated kidneys are needed than are available each year. For further information, contact the National Kidney Foundation, 2 Park Avenue, New York, NY 10016; 212-889-2210, or the Kidney Foundation of Canada, Suite 555, 4060 St. Catherine Street West, Montreal, QC H3Z 2Z3; 800-361-7994. Consult local telephone directories or national offices for addresses of local branches.

Blood. This is the most commonly "transplanted" tissue, with some twelve million transfusions occurring annually in the United States alone. Voluntary donor blood has become adequate to meet current needs, and the use of commercial blood has been discontinued. There has been talk of using cadaver blood. It costs more to extract, but the cost of testing is much lower, due to the larger amount taken from the donor. If the procedure for extracting it can be improved, it could become an extremely valuable resource. Significant economies in testing would result from the need for only one test on a large volume of blood. The cost of blood testing is rising. Blood is now tested for syphilis, the AIDS virus, the HTLV-1 virus, and various forms of hepatitis. While the tests are not a hundred percent reliable, the chance of getting an infection through blood transfusion is now a tiny fraction of one percent. For total safety the patient's own blood can, when practical, be stored for subsequent use during surgery. For further information, contact the Blood Services Laboratories, American Red Cross, 15601 Crabbs Branch Way, Rockville, MD 20855, or Blood Transfusion Service, The Canadian Red Cross Society, 1800 Alta Vista Drive, Ottawa, ON, K1G 4J5.

Ear Tissues. Persons over age five (no upper age limit), even those with nerve-related hearing impairments, can bequeath middle ear tissue to restore hearing to as many as six people with conductive hearing loss. Cause of death must be provided with donation. The Ear Bank of Project HEAR has provided over 25,000 ear implants since 1969. For further information, contact Project HEAR, 801 Welch Rd., Palo Alto, CA 94304; 415-494-2000. In Canada the Ontario Temporal Bone Bank is gone but there is now the Ear Bank of British Columbia, 865 W. 10th Ave., Vancouver, BC V5Z 1L7; 604-876-3211 / 3212. Conducts research and supplies temporal bones and tympanic membranes for transplant. Solicits tissues from both normal and impaired. Requests medical histories.

Ear Tissues for Research. As above, persons with hearing problems or ear disorders are urged to bequeath ear structures for research, along with a medical history from the donor's doctor. Removal of ear structures (a specialized task) is arranged in the United States by the National Temporal Bone Banks Center of the Deafness Research Foundation, 9 E. 38th St., New York, NY 10016.

Livers. There were 4,698 livers transplanted in the United States in 1999, and as of June, 2000, 115,556 patients were waiting.

Hearts. In 1999, there were 2,185 heart transplants in the United States. As of June, 2000, there were 4,123 Americans waiting for heart transplants, plus another 207 waiting for heart-lung transplants.

Brain Tissue. Postmortem research into Alzheimer's disease, Parkinson's disease, epilepsy, multiple sclerosis, and other disorders involving brain pathology is being conducted with donated brain and other nerve tissue. Normal brain tissue is also urgently needed for this research. Contact the Canadian Brain Tissue Bank, Room 127, Banting Institute, 100 College Street, Toronto, ON M5G 1L5; 416-977-3398, or the Brain Tissue Resource Center, Ralph Lowell Laboratories, Harvard Medical School, 115 Mill St., Belmont, MA 02178; 617-855-2400.

Pancreases. In 1999, 363 pancreases alone were transplanted in the United States and in 2000, 921 people were waiting for such transplants, and another 2,328 for combination kidney-pancreas transplants. In a new development, a rapidly increasing number of patients are awaiting pancreas islet cells, following breakthrough medical discoveries in Canada that may lead to a cure for Type 1 diabetes.

Lungs. In 1999 there were 885 lung transplants and 49 heart-lung transplants in the United States. In 2000, there were 3,640 patients waiting for lung transplants and 207 more waiting for heart-lung transplants.

Other Organs. Many other tissues are valuable in promoting health and saving lives—among them cartilage, iliac crests, dura mater, fascia lata, joints, intestines, and bone marrow.

Artificial Implants. Postmortem donation of devices such as pacemakers, bone wire and screws, joints, and other artificial implants, with permission to analyze related tissues, can be extremely helpful for research on how such implants perform and interact with human tissue once in place.

Eyeglasses. In the United States, eyeglasses may be donated to New Eyes for the Needy, Box 332, 549 Millburn Ave., Short Hills, NJ 07078; 201-376-4093, which receives and distributes them through medical missions and hospitals overseas. Sale of donated jewelry and precious metal scrap (gold dental crowns, eyeglass frames, earrings, etc.) fund new eyeglasses for U.S. recipients. In Canada, eyeglasses may be sent to Operation Eyesight Universal, 4 Parkdale Cr. NW, Calgary, Alta. T2N 3T8; 403-283-6323.

BEQUEATHAL OF BODIES TO MEDICAL SCHOOLS

The Need for Donations. Bequeathals are increasing, but not fast enough. Also, greater sharing is needed between areas of surplus and shortage. The degree of need in any medical school may change from time to time. It is wise, therefore, to check with nearby medical schools in advance and, if possible, to file bequeathal papers with the school before death occurs. Donors with papers on file will take precedence over those who have not filed in advance. If you wish the cremains returned, check with the medical school. Most, but not all, are glad to do this.

Alternative Plans. It is important to have an alternative plan, preferably through a local funeral consumer organization, in case a body is not accepted by a medical school. Some schools are amply supplied or may decline a bequeathal because of the condition of the body. A body may be rejected if it is mutilated or autopsied, or if organs other than eyes have been removed. Likewise, contagious diseases, systemic infections, obesity, and other medical conditions *may* disqualify a body for medical school use. Check with your local medical school, as schools vary in their requirements and change from time to time.

Procedures at Time of Death. If bequeathal papers are on file, call the school(s) to make arrangements. If papers have not been filed, consult the directory of medical schools following this section and call the nearest school that accepts bequeathals. If the body is accepted, it may be removed immediately to the school if there is to be no service in the presence of the body, as when a memorial service is held instead of a funeral service.

If the body is to be held for viewing or a service, or sent by common carrier, the funeral director should consult the medical school for instructions. If embalming is done, special procedures must be used, as ordinary embalming will disqualify a body for medical school.

UNIFORM DONOR CARD

Transportation of the Remains. The body may be delivered in a private vehicle, or by a funeral director. If no funeral director is used, someone else must handle the legal papers. In warm weather, the body should be taken to the school within twenty-four hours, unless refrigeration (which can be by dry ice) or embalming is used. If the body is to be delivered by common carrier, it must be prepared by a funeral director. Some medical schools pay no transportation expenses. Most pay the expense within the state or within a certain radius. *See the Medical School Directory.* Expenses beyond that distance are paid by the family. Incidentally, Amtrak offers fast, cheap service to some three hundred destinations.

A Deeply Meaningful Experience. The family may prefer to take the body to the medical school themselves, using a station wagon. This has been the practice in our family, and we would not think of turning it over to someone else. It is something we can do for the loved one and helps us to accept the loss. The body may be placed in a box or on a stretcher or a plain canvas cot, or simply wrapped in a blanket. People are repelled by death and often shrink from handling a dead body. In practice, however, the privilege of helping to care for the body of a friend or a loved one is a deeply meaningful experience. Too often in modern life we withdraw from reality or call in a professional to do things we might benefit by doing for ourselves.

Legal Papers. While the legal procedures in our state are simple, this varies from state to state. See Chapter 5, "Simple Burial and Cremation," the Transporting of Bodies section.

Message to Recipients. I am attaching the following message to my bequeathal form and related documents, to be delivered to the students who will be making use of my body, subject to the approval of the dean of the anatomy department, and signed only "The Donor:"

I am pleased that my body may, after my death, be of service to humankind in the training of doctors. This opportunity adds a creative dimension to my death and I appreciate your helping to make it possible.
—*The Donor*

MEDICAL SCHOOLS OF CANADA AND THE UNITED STATES

This information was compiled with the help of the schools of medicine, dentistry and osteopathy in the United States, Canada and Puerto Rico. It includes the degree of need of each school for the bequeathal of bodies and the distance, if any, from which the school will pay transportation. The list is in geo-alphabetical sequence.

Key to this directory:

DEGREE OF NEED	TRANSPORTATION PAID
U - Urgent Need	*W/C* - Within County
M - Urgent Need	*W/S* - Within State
A - Supplies ample	*W/P* - Within Province
N - No bequeathals	*150 mi* - Within that radius
needed	*Local* - Local area only
	None - No transportation paid

Canadian Medical Schools

U. of Calgary, Faculty of Medicine, 3330 Hospital Dr. NW, Calgary AB T2N 4N1
403-220-6848 U $250.

U. of Alberta, Faculty of Med., 5-14 Med. Sci. Bldg., Edmonton AB T6G 2H7
403-492-2203 U None

Dept. of Anat., Fac. of Med., #317 - 2197 Health Sc. Mall, Instruc. Resources Ctr., U. of B.C., Vancouver BC V6T 1Z3
604-822-2578/876-2161 A Local

U. of Manitoba, Human Anat. & Cell. Sc., 730 William Ave.,Winnipeg MB R3E 0W3
204-789-3652 M $60

Memorial U., Faculty of Med., Prince Philip Drive, St. John's NF A1B 3V6
709-737-6727 U W/P

Dalhousie U., Faculty of Med., Tupper Medical Bldg., Halifax NS B3H 4H7
902-494-2051 A W/P (Mar.)

McMaster U., Anatomy Program, 1200 Main St. W., Hamilton ON L8N 3Z5
905-525-9140 M Local

Queen's U., Faculty of Med., Dept. of Anatomy, Kingston ON K7L 3N6
613-545-2600 N None

U. of Western Ontario, Fac. of Medicine, Dept. of Anat., Richmond St., London ON N6A 5C1   519-661-3014/2075 M None

U. of Ottawa, Anat. Dept., Hlth. Sci. Ctr, 451 Smyth Rd., Ottawa ON K1H 8M5
613-562-5414; fax 562-5464 A None

U. of Toronto, Dept. of Anatomy and Cell Biology, Med. Sciences Bldg., Toronto ON M5S 1A8   416-978-2692 M None

McGill U., Dept. of Anatomy, 3640 Univ. St., Montreal QC. H3A 2B2
514-398-6335 M Local

U. de Montreal, Dept. of Anatomy and Cell Biology, Pavillon principal R-816, 2900 Boulevard Edouard-Montpetit, C.P. 6128 Succ. "A", Montreal QC H3C 3J7
514-343-6288 M 100 mi

U. de Sherbrooke, Fac. de Medecine, Departement D'Anatomie, Sherbrooke QC J1H 5N4 819-563-5555/564-5271 U Local

Univ. of Saskatchewan, College of Medicine, Dept. of Anat., Saskatoon SK S7N 0W0
306-966-4075 M W/P

U.S. Medical Schools

Anatomy Board of Puerto Rico, Med. Sci. Bldg., 5th Fl. #503, San Juan PR 00936
800-758-2525×1510 U W/PR

U. of Alabama, Dept. of Cell Biology & Anatomy, UAB Station, Birmingham AL 35294   205-934-4494 M Local

U. of So. Alabama, Structural & Cellular Biol., 2042 Med. Sciences Bldg., Mobile AL 36688   334-460-6764 M None

U. of Arizona, Coll. of Med., Dept. of Cell. Biology & Anat., Tucson AZ 85724-5044
602-626-6084 M 25 mi

U. of Ark., Coll. of Med., Anat. Dept., Little Rock AR 72205   501-686-5180 A 50 mi

U. of California, Davis., Dept. of Cell Bio. & Human Anatomy, School of Medicine, Rm. 3301, Davis, CA 95616-8643.
916-752-2100 M 30 mi

U.C. at Irvine, Dept. of Anatomy & Neurobiology, College of Med., Irvine CA 92717
213-856-6061 U Local

U.C. at San Diego, Sch. of Med., Learning Resources Office, La Jolla CA 92093
619-534-4536 M W/C

Loma Linda U., Anat. Dept., Loma Linda CA 92350   714-824-4301 M None

U.C. at L.A., Dept. of Anatomy & Cell Biology, School of Med., Los Angeles CA 90024   909-825-9563 M 50 mi

U. of So. Calif. School of Med., 1333 San Pablo St. Los Angeles CA 90033
213-222-0231 M 50 mi

Calif. State Polytechnic Univ., 3801 West Temple Ave., Pomona CA 91768
213-869-4038 N 50 mi

State Curator of N. Calif. U. of C. at S.F., Sch. of Med., Anatomy Dept., San Francisco CA 94143-0902
415-476-1981 M None

Div. of Human Anat., Stanford U. Med. School, Stanford CA 94305-5065
415-723-2404 U 75 mi

U. of Colorado, School of Med., 4200 E. 9th Ave., B-111, Denver CO 80262
303-270-8554/399-1211 M None

U. of Conn. Health Ctr., Farmington Ave., Farmington CT 06032
203-223-4340 U W/S

Yale U. School of Medicine, Dept. of Surgery, Sec. of Gross Anatomy, 333 Cedar St., P.O. Box 3333, New Haven CT 06510
203-785-2813 M W/S

Georgetown U. Medical Ctr., Dept. of Cell Biology, 3900 Reservoir Rd NW, Washington DC 20007
202-687-1219/0100 after hours A 50 mi

Howard U., College of Med., Dept. of Anatomy, Washington DC 20059
202-636-6555 A Local

Geo. Washington U., Anat. Dept., 2300 I St. NW, Washington DC 20037
202-994-3511 U W/S

Anatomical Bd. of Fla., U. of Fla., Coll. of Med., Gainesville FL 32610
352-392-3588 / 800-628-2594 M None

U. of Miami, School of Med., Dept. of Cell Bio & Anatomy, P.O. Box 016960, Miami FL 33101   305-547-6691 M None

Anat. Dept., Coll. of Med., U. of S. FL, 12901 Bruce B. Downs Blvd., Tampa FL 33612   813-974-2843 A None

Emory U. School of Med., Dept. of Anatomy & Cell Biology, Atlanta GA 30322
          404-727-6242 M None

Morehouse School of Medicine, 720 Westview Dr., SW, Atlanta GA 30310
          404-752-1560/1500 M 50 mi

Med. Coll. of Ga., School of Med., Anatomy Dept., 1120 15th St., Augusta GA 30912
          404-721-3731 M W/S

Mercer U. School of Med., 1550 College St., Macon GA 31207
          912-752-4013 A 70 mi

U. of Hawaii, Dept. of Anatomy & Repro. Biol., 1960 East-West Rd., Honolulu HI 96822   808-956-7131/800-734-5283
          fax 956-9481 M W/C

Anatomical Gift Assn. of Ill., 2240 W. Fillmore, Chicago IL 60612
          312-733-5283 U None

Indiana Univ., Anatomical Educ. Program, Rm. 259, Med. Sc. Bldg., 635 Barnhill Dr, Indianapolis IN 46202-5120
          317-274-7450 M W/S $200

Univ. of Osteopathic Med. & Health Sci., 3200 Grand Ave., Des Moines IA 50312
          515-271-1481 M W/S

U. of Iowa, Coll. of Med., Dept. of Anatomy, Iowa City IA 152242
          319-335-7762 A None

U. of Kansas Medical Center, Dept. of Anatomy & Cell Biology, 39th & Rainbow Blvd., Kan. City KS 66185
          913-588-7000 M None

U. of Kentucky Body Bequeathal Prog., MN 224 Med. Ctr., Lexington KY 40536-0084
          606-323-5160 U Central & E. KY

U. of Louisville Sch. of Med., Health Sciences Center, Dept. of Anatomical Sciences & Neurobiology, Louisville KY 40292
          502-582-5165 M Local

Bureau of Anatomical Svcs., Dept. of Anat., 1901 Perdido St., New Orleans LA 70112-1393
          504-568-4012/
          504-588-5255 A W/S & MS coast

U. of New England, Coll. of Osteopathic Med., 11 Hills Beach Rd., Biddeford ME 04005   207-283-0171 A 500 mi

State Anat. Bd., 655 W. Baltimore, Rm. B-026 Baltimore MD 21201
          410-547-1222/800-879-2728 M W/S

Uniformed Services, Univ. of the Health Sciences, 4301 Jones Bridge Road, Bethesda MD 20814-4799
          301-295-3333 U 150 mi

U. Mass. Med. Sch., Anat. Gift Program, 55 Lake Ave. N., Worcester MA 01605
          508-856-2460 A W/S

U. of Mich. Anat. Dontns. Prog., 3626 Med. Sc. Bldg. II, Ann Arbor MI 48109-0616
          313-764-4359 U None

Wayne State U. Sch. of Med., Anatomy Dept. 540 E. Canfield, Detroit MI 48201
          313-577-1188/1198 M Local

Mich. State U., Anatomy Dept. E. Lansing MI 48824
          517-353-5398/355-1855 A Local

U. of Minn. Coll. of Med. Sc., Anatomy Bequest Program, 4-144 Jackson Hall, 321 Church St., Minneapolis MN 55455
          612-625-1111 M Local

U. of Miss. Medical Center, 2500 N. State St., Jackson MS 39216
          601-984-1000 M 300 mi

*In Missouri, make bequeathals to individual schools, or to:*Missouri State Anatomical Bd., Dept. of Anatomy & Neurology, School of Med., U. of MO, Columbia MO 65212
          314-882-2288 M None

Anatomical Bd. of Nebraska, 600 S. 42nd St., Omaha NE 68105
402-559-6249 A 250 mi

Dept. of Anatomy, U. of Nev., Sch. of Med., Reno NV 89557-0046
702-784-6113 A W/S

Anatomical Gifts Program, Dept. of Anatomy, Dartmouth Medical School, Hanover NH 03755-3832
603-650-1636 M W/S & VT

U. of Med. and Dentistry of NJ, NJ Med. Sch., 185 S. Orange Ave. Newark NJ 07103
201-456-4648 M W/S

UMDNJ, School of Osteopathic Medicine, 40 Laurel Rd., Stratford NJ 08084
604-346-7050 A W/S

UMDNJ-Robert Wood Johnson Med. Sch., Anatomical Assn., 675 Hoes Lane, Piscataway NJ 08854
800-GIFT-211 M None

Univ. of N.M., Anatomy Dept., North Campus, Albuquerque NM 87131
505-277-2555 M W/S

Anat. Gift Prog., Dept. of Anat., Albany Medical College, 47 New Scotland Ave, Albany NY 12208
518-362-5379 M 120 mi

State U. of N.Y., Health Sc. Ctr at Brooklyn, M.A. Kahn, MD, PhD, Dir. of Anatomy, Box 5, 450 Clarkson Ave., Brooklyn NY 11203
212-270-1014/3890 U 100 mi

State U. of NY at Buffalo, Sch. of Med., Anat. Sciences Dept., Attn. Dr. R. Dannenhoffer, 317 Farber Hall, Buffalo NY 14214
716-824-2912 M 100 mi

Columbia U. Coll. of Physicians & Surgeons, 630 W. 168th St., New York NY 10032
212-305-3451 U 150 mi

Cornell U. Med. Coll., 1300 York Ave., New York NY 10021
212-746-6140 U 90 mi

Mt. Sinai Medical Ctr., One Gustave L. Levy Pl., New York NY 10029
212-241-7057 M 150 mi

N.Y. Univ., Dept. of Cellular Biology, Anatomy Dept. Attn. Dr. Bogart, 550 First Ave., New York NY 10016
212-340-5378 U 50 mi

Yeshiva U., Albert Einstein Coll. of Med., Dept. Anatomy & Struct. Biology, 1300 Morris Park Ave., Bronx, NY 10461
718-430-3142 U Local

U. of Rochester Sch. of Med., Anat. Gift Prog., 601 Elmwood Ave., Rochester NY 14642   716-275-2592/2272 M Local

Dept. of Anat. Sciences, Sch. of Med., Health Sci. Ctr., SUNY at Stony Brook, Stony Brook NY 11794   516-444-3111
U Nassau & Suffolk Counties

State U of NY Health Sc. Ctr.-Syracuse, Dept. of Anat & Cell Biol., 766 Irving Ave., Syracuse NY 13210 315-464-5120 U W/S

N.Y. Med. Coll., Basic Sc. Bldg., Valhalla NY 10595   914-594-4025/4226 U 50 mi

Medical Sciences Teaching Labs, Attn: Manfred Phelps, U of NC, CB#7520, Berryhill Hall, Chapel Hill NC 27599-7520
919-966-1134 U if needed

Dept. of Biological Anthropology & Anat., Box 3170, Duke Med. Ctr., Anat. Dept., Box 3170, Durham NC 27710
919-684-4124 M
W/S (for indigent families)

E. Carolina U., Sch. of Med., Anatomy & Cell Biology Dept., Greenville NC 27858-4354   919-816-2843 M East NC

Bowman Gray Sch. of Med., Winston-Salem NC 27103   919-716-4368 A None

U. of North Dakota Sch. of Med., Anatomy Dept., Grand Forks ND 58202
701-777-2101 M W/S

Ohio U. College of Osteopathic Med., Rm. #135, Grosvenor Hall, Athens OH 45701-2979   614-593-1800/594-2416 M W/S

U. of Cincinnati Coll. of Med., Cincinnati OH 45267-0521   513-558-5612 M None

Case Western Reserve Med. Sch. 2109 Adelbert Rd., Cleveland OH 44106
215-368-3430/221-9330 M 75 mi

Ohio State U., Dept. of Cell Biology, 4072 Graves Hall, 333 W. 10th Ave., Columbus OH 43210-1239   614-292-4831 A None

Wright State U., Sch. of Med., Donated Body Prog., Anat. Dept., Dayton OH 45435
513-873-3066 A Local

NE Ohio Univ. Coll. of Med., P.O. Box 95, Rootstown OH 44272
330-325-2511×255 M 75 mi

Med. Coll. of Ohio at Toledo, P.O. 10008, 3000 Arlington Ave., Toledo OH 43699-0008   419-381-4172 M None

U. of Okla. Health Sci. Ctr, Box 26901, Rm 100-BSEB, Attn. Pam Lawson, Okla. City OK 73190   405-271-2424 M W/S

Coll. of Osteopathic Med. of Okla. State Univ., 1111 W. 17th St., Tulsa OK 74107
918-582-1972 M 100 mi

Oregon Hlth. Sci. Univ., Sch. of Med., Anatomy Dept., Portland OR 97201
503-494-8302/7811 U None

Humanity Gifts Registry of Pa., P.O. Box 835, Philadelphia PA 19105-0835
215-922-4440 U W/S $50

Brown Univ., Helen Shuman, Box-G, Div. of Biology & Medicine, Providence RI 02912   401-863-9029 U 150 mi

Medical University of S.C., Dept. of Anatomy & Cell Biology, Dr. Donald R. DiBona, 171 Ashley Ave., Charleston SC 29425
803-792-3521 M W/S

Univ. of S.D. School of Medicine, Vermillion SD 57069
605-677-5321/624-3932 U 150 mi

E. Tenn. State U., James H. Quillen Coll. of Med., Anat. Dept., Box 70582, Johnson City TN 37614-0582
423-439-6241 M 30 mi

U. of Tenn. Ctr. for Health Sci. 875 Monroe Ave., Memphis TN 38163
901-448-5965 (bus. hrs.)/ 901-448-5500(24 hrs.) U W/S*

Meharry Med. Coll., 1005 Todd Blvd., Nashville TN 37208
615-327-6288/6289 U W/S

Vanderbilt U. Sch. of Med., Vanderbilt Anat. Donation Prog., 201 Light Hall, Nashville TN 37232-0685
615-322-7948 M 50 mi

Tex. A&M U. Med. Coll., Anat. Dept., College Station TX 77843
409-845-4913/822-1571 A 100 mi

Baylor Coll. of Dent. Anat. Dept., 3302 Gaston Ave., Dallas TX 75246
214-828-8270/8290 M 200 mi

U. of Tex. Southwestern Medical Center at Dallas, Div. of Anatomy, 5323 Harry Hines Blvd., Dallas TX 75235-9039
214-688-2221/2232 A 150 mi

U.N.T. Health Science Center at Fort Worth, Dept. of Anat. & Cell Biology, 3500 Camp Bowie Blvd., Ft. Worth TX 76107-2690
817-735-2045 M 50 mi

Willed Body Program, U. of Texas, Med. Branch, Galveston TX 77550-1308
100 772 1203 M 300 mi

Baylor Coll. of Medicine, 1 Baylor Plaza, Houston TX 77030
713-798-4930 A 100 mi

U. of Tex. Health Sci. Ctr. at Houston, P.O. Box 20708, Houston TX 77225
713-500-5603 A 250 mi

---

*U of Tenn pays for preliminary embalming and transportation within state, if donor has filed a bequest prior to death. Accept donations initiated by the next-of-kin following death only when expenses are prepaid by the estate. For next-of-kin gifts, the payment requirement is waived if death occurs in the local area (Shelby County).

Texas Tech. U. Health Sc. Ctr., Anatomy Dept., Lubbock TX 79430
806-743-2700/3111 M 360 mi

U. of Tex. Health Sci. Ctr., 7703 Floyd Curl Dr., San Antonio TX 78284-7762
210-567-3900 A 100 mi

U. of Utah, Sch. of Med., Anat. Dept., Salt Lake City UT 84132
801-581-6728/2121 U 50 mi

U. of Vt., Coll. of Med., Dept. of Anat. & Neurobio., Burlington VT 05405
802-656-2230/3131 A None

E. Va. Med. School, Anat. Dept., Box 1980, Norfolk VA 23501
757-446-5640/786-2479 A W/S

State Anatomical Div., Dept of Health, Richmond VA 23219
804-786-2479/3174 A W/S

U. of Wash. Dept. of Biological Structure, Sch. of Med., Box 357420, Seattle WA 98195   206-543-1860 M Local

Marshall U. School of Medicine, Huntington WV 25755-9350   304-696-7382 A W/S

W.V.S1.O.M., Human Gift Registry, 400 N. Lee St., Lewisburg WV 24901
304-645-6270 M W/S

WV Univ., Human Gift Registry, Morgantown WV 26506   304-293-6322 A 150 mi

U. of Wisc. Med. Sch., Anat. Dept., 325 SMI, Madison WI 53706
608-262-2888 M W/S

The Med. Coll. of Wisc., Dept. of Cellular Biology and Anatomy, Attn: Dr. S. Kaplan, 8701 Watertown Plank Rd., Milwaukee WI 53226   414-257-8261/8262 M None

ENDNOTE

[1]Canadian statistics are from the Health Services and Promotion Branch, Health and Welfare Canada, Ottawa, Ontario K1A 1B4. U.S. figures are from the United Network for Organ Sharing.

INDEX